Outbursts!

OUTBURSTS!
A QUEER EROTIC THESAURUS

A.D PETERKIN

Arsenal Pulp Press
Vancouver

ARSENAL PULP PRESS
103 - 1014 Homer Street
Vancouver, B.C.
Canada V6B 2W9
arsenalpulp.com

The publisher gratefully acknowledges the support of the Government of Canada through the Book
Publishing Industry Development Program for its publishing activities.

Interior design by Robert Ballantyne
Editorial assistance by Trish Kelly
Cover design by russty-b
Cover photography by Brett McEwen and Senkowski Photographic
Title page photography by Dianne Whelan
Printed and bound in Canada

National Library of Canada
Cataloguing in Publication Data

Peterkin, Allan D
Outbursts! : a queer erotic thesaurus / A.D. Peterkin.

Includes bibliographical references.
ISBN 1-55152-151-2

1. Gays--Language--Dictionaries. 2. Sex--Dictionaries. 3. English
language--Slang--Dictionaries. I. Title.

HQ79.13.P47 2003   306.76'6'03   C2003-911209-8

INTRODUCTION

Compiling a thesaurus of queer erotic terms is not quite like writing *The Bald-Headed Hermit and the Artichoke,* my first erotic thesaurus.[1] Gays, lesbians or other queers have developed separate and at times secret codes and terms to describe their sexualities and proclivities. But while you won't find, "husband" or "wife" here, there are many similarities; as with straight erotic terms, many use rhyming, alliteration, acronyms, abbreviations and other languages as sources, and often words are shared. As well, many terms, mostly derogatory, are inspired by non-queer, hateful, and often xenophobic notions.

Certainly, a good number of the words listed in this book under "penis," for example, are gay-specific, but a cock is still understood to be a cock. And yet, even though a gay man is likely to figure that "child-getter" is a synonym for penis, not many would ever place a personal ad bragging possession of "8 inches of child-getter." Then again, queer language is in a state of near-constant flux, much in keeping with the ever increasing visibility of gays and lesbians in contemporary culture, and a growing acceptance (by both gays and straights) of the validity of queer sexuality in all its guises. Pick up a lesbian erotica anthology more than ten years old and try to find a reference to "girl-cock." Skim that same book for a story where a woman calls her partner's genitals "pussy." You'll find neither.

In earlier, more dangerous times, men and women needed to create secret "passwords" in order to identify one another, to see whether the code was returned. One result of this pressure to invent was the secret male language called Polari (more or less from "parlare," to speak in Italian), used by gay men in London from the 1930s to 1970s. The language of Polari contained some 500 words about sex, the body, physical appearance, meeting places, straights and gays. (Examples can be found throughout *Outbursts!*)

Although Polari never spread far past the British Isles and is now concidered obsolete, it's a good example of the creative results produced under the pressure to invent a sexual language of one's own (if "one" can be meant to describe an entire covert community). Some Polari terms, like "bod," "trade," "troll," "basket," and "cottage," are still used today, and many have been absorbed into mainstream vocabulary as well.

We are, in many ways, more liberated than ever before in Western culture. Though gays and lesbians can now enjoy its advancements, an entire generation of queers has come of age without memory of life before the Gay Liberation movement or even the beginning of the AIDS crisis in the early 1980s.[2] Still, the desire to codify, to create lingo with real verve—that only our peers will get—remains particularly as gay and lesbian sexual "factions" desire identities of their own. As an example, in the 1990s, we saw the emergence of bear culture and terminology to describe hirsute, physically large gay men and their admirers.[2] For a complete Bear manifesto and glossary on loving all things gay, hairy, and cuddly, see the website *www.sanfranciscobear.com*.[3]

The Internet itself has been a large influence on queer erotic language. Chat rooms and online personal ads have led to an entire subgenre of acronyms for queer desires and sensibilities. At the same time, the many personalized websites with gay slang dictionaries and lists have given us insight into the variations in the meaning of queer terms in local communities. The 1990s also saw published works by transgendered activists like Kate Bornstein and Leslie Feinberg that radicalized how gay mainstream culture talks about gender. Such discussions highlight some of the shortcomings of gay and lesbian erotic language, much of which has been inherited for the straight world. We can see this in the relative brevity of sections relating to women, as well as in the fetichizing terms for non-white queers. As the "catch-up" takes place, more and different words appear, but you will see, for example, that the section for "vagina" is still small compared to the lengthy section for "penis." This is a problem left over from the vestiges of the phallocentric society that still requires redress. Or is it? Is it necessary for there to be a future where lesbians have just as many words for "pussy" and "cunnilingus" as gay men have for "cock" and "fellatio"? Perhaps our goals when describing our erotic lives are not identical or universal.

Consider the case of "butch" or "femme." The meaning of these terms is heavily dependent on the speaker. Spoken by a straight man, butch or femme can be perjorative, a commentary on the presence or absence of masculinity and the power it affords.

Sometimes words are shared by gay men and lesbians, but even when words are shared, their meanings may not be. When a queer woman is described as being "butch," often what is being described is the behaviours that reveal her queerness. Conversely, a gay man who behaves "butch" is often concealing his queerness.

Where the meanings of the word "butch" overlap is in their nod to the fact that we assume this role, or as queer theorist Judith Butler explains, we perform it. This is something that we understand better than straights, before them, probably because most of us have felt ourselves "performing" straightness at some point.[4] The thrill of performance, whether it conceals our queerness or reveals it openly, is a subtext to much of the queer erotic language.

How is queer language different from straight language? It is a difficult question to answer. Even the word "queer" itself sparks controversy. For some men and women in the gay community, the word carries very negative memories of growing up when the word "queer" was a condemnation that dangerously stamped you as Other. For younger members of gay culture, it is associated with queer theory and a radical politic that strives to ally gays, lesbians, bis, trans people, and other disenfranchised minorities under one umbrella. In his essay "Identity and Politics in a 'Postmodern' Gay Culture," Steven Seidman says, "gay liberation is more than a movement to liberate eros; it is a gender revolution."[5] It is not just a struggle for the freedom to bed who we want to bed. It is also a struggle to name what we do in bed, who we are in bed, who we take with us to bed. So while the word "queer" comes with a lot of baggage and connotations, it is also an excellent example of what the words in this book tend to do.

The terms you'll find in *Outbursts!* are often challenging. They insist there is a sophistication to our desire, a sense of humour, a complexity, an ability to take even the most perjorative, nastily implied word and do exactly whatever we want with it. Many of the words in this book have taken on new meanings, and some still ring hateful like a taunt in the schoolyard or street, but they have been included here perhaps as a dare. Whatever the case, take these words and do what you want with them—they've been very naughty.

—A.D. Peterkin

1. Peterkin, A.D. *The Bald-Headed Hermit and the Artichoke: An Erotic Thesaurus.* Vancouver: Arsenal Pulp Press, 2000.

2. Marcus, Eric, *Making Gay History.* New York: HarperCollins, 1992.

3. Les Wright, *www.sanfranciscobear.com*

4. Butler, Judith. *Gender Trouble: Feminism and the Subversion of Identity.* New York: Routledge, 1990.

5. Seidman, Steven. "Identity and Politics in a 'Postmodern' Gay Culture." In *Fear of a Queer Planet.* Ed. Michael Warner. Minneapolis: University of Minnesota Press, 1993. p. 113.

Swami talked about Ramakrishna (19th-century Indian avatar of Godhead, sometime transvestite and coquette) and Girish Ghosh (poet and drinker). They once had a competition to find out which of them knew the bigger number of risqué words. (It was amusing to hear this corny French adjective pop up out of Swami's vocabulary.) Afer they had both said all the risqué words they knew. Girish bowed down and told Ramakrishna. "You are my guru in this also."

—Christopher Isherwood, *My Guru and His Disciple*

Abdomen

SEE ALSO MUSCULAR

A ripped muscular abdomen has become a sexual status symbol and a source of obsession for millions of body-conscious men and women today.

Abdominal Snowman, abs, alvus, Aunt Nelly, bay window, bazoo, belly, bingy/binjy, corporation, front porch, fuck handles, gizzard, goodyear, gut(s), landing pad, love handles, Maconochie, mid-section, middle, midriff Mary, Ned Kelly, Newingbus, paunch, pot belly, shit locker, six-pack, spare tire, stomach, tum-tum, tummy, washboard

Abdominal Snowman: a guy with great abs.
Abs: what everyone wants but few of us have.
Maconochie: from the name of a well-known tinned stew in England.

Anal Sex: SEE SODOMY

Androgyne

SEE ALSO EFFEMINATE, BISEXUAL, TRANSEXUAL, TRANSGENDERED

An archaic term for an individual with blurred gender identification.

ambisexual, bisexual, epicene, gynandrous, hermaphrodite, Jenny Willocks, John and Joan, moff, morphadite, morphodite, pantrope, Pat, scrat, shim, will-gill

Pat: the Saturday Night Live *gender-blurry geek.*
Morphadite/morphodite: evolved from hermaphrodite, *who in Greek mythology was the child of Hermes and Aphrodite, depicted as bisexual.*

Anus

SEE ALSO BUTTOCKS, SODOMY, SODOMIZE, SODOMITE

Like a mauve carnation puckered up
and dim it breathes, meekly nestled
amid the foam
damp, too from caresses tracing the
smooth dome

of creamy buttocks up to the innermost
rim.
— *"Sonnet to the Asshole," by Paul Verlaine and Arthur Rimbaud*

A-hole, A double S, abyss, arris, ars, ars musica, arse, ass, asshole, asscrack, azz, back porch, backdoor, backeye, backeye slice, backeye slit, backhole, backs, backway, bahookie, ballinocack, balley goods, barking spider, bazoo, beauts, beautocks, beauty, big hole, blind eye, birdcage, biting dog,

Biting dog: a tightening of the anal sphincter muscle.
Boy pussy: 20th-century American gay slang.
Bullhead: a virginal ass. Also: cherry.

blot, blurter, bon bons, bogy, boody, booty, bottle and glass, boy cunt, boy pussy, broad, bronze eye, brown, brown cherry, brown daisy, brown eye, brown house, brown lips, brown Windsor, brownie, Brunswick, brown towel holder, bucket, buckeye, bullhead, bum, bum bucket, bumhole, bunghole, bun-bun, bunky, bunt, butthole, Cadbury cul-de-sac, canetta, change machine, chips, chocolate buttonhole, chocolate starfish, chocolate speedway, chudini, chuff, chutney locker, codeye, cooze, copper penny, coops, corn-dot, cornhole, council gritter, crack, culo, cozy drop, daisy dot, date, date locker, deadeye, dinger, dirt box, dirt chute, dirt factory, dirt hole, ditch, dish, dopey, dot, dung-trumper, duster, elephant and castle, exhaust pipe, eye, farthole, feak, freckle, fruit/froot loops, fuck passage, fudge pipes, fugo, fun, garage, gates, gazoo, gazool, gee-gee/gigi, gig, glass asshole, glory hole, gonga, gooseberry grinder, gooseberry maker, gripples/grippley, grand canyon,

Dish: Polari for anus.
Elephant and castle: rhymes somewhat with asshole.
Glass asshole: a hairless anus.
Grand canyon: a widely used hole.

Hawaiian eye, ham, Helmet Cole, Hershey Highway, hind-boot,

hinder entrance, hole, Hollywood uterus, honey roles, hoop, jacks, jacksie/jacksy, jampot, jock hole, kazoo, keister, khaki pussy, Khyber Pass, kwazakoo, leather, lovebubb, lunar sanctum, man pussy, mangina,

Khyber Pass: a 19th-century English term; an example of rhyming slang (in this case rhyming with ass).
Khaki pussy: a military man's ass.
Natural breech: an over-stretched anus, referring obliquely to childbirth.

marmite motorway, medlar, monocular eye-glass, muck spreader, muddy starfish, mud-eye, mustard pot, nachas, nancy, natural breech, nockandro, north pole, o-ring, ort, Paliass, pan, pockeroo, podex, poo hatch, poo percolator, poon, poop chute, poophole, porthole, prison pucker hole, pussy, quoit, raisin, rear end, rear entrance, recky, rec-tum, rinctum,

Paliass: Polari for anus (and an operatic homonym).
Poop (for buttocks): dates to 17th-century England and derives from the back of a ship.
Poophole and poop chute came to refer to the anus.
Slack Alva: an overused, loose anus.
Shut butt: a tight anal sphincter.

ring, ring piece, rip, rosebud, round eye, round mouth, saddle, satchel, scratch, second eye, servant's entrance, sewer, shit chute, shithole, shitter, shut butt, siege, slack Alva, slop chute, sphincter, spice island, stank, stench trench, tan track, tassel, tip, tokus, tradesman's entrance, trill, turkish delight, twatarooney, up your gary glitter (up your shitter), V/A (virgin ass), web center, where the sun don't shine, windmill, windward passage, winker-stinker, zero

Aphrodisiac

SEE ALSO PARAPHERNALIA

This list includes synonyms as well as examples of substances thought to enhance sexual response and performance, including foods and roots.

absinthe, Amyl, aroma, aroma of man, asparagus, back up pills, bear gall-bladder, bird's nest soup, Butyl, caviar, celery, cinnamon, charm, cocaine, delay cream, disc cleaner, E (Ecstasy), Ex (Ecstasy), fennel, GHB, ginseng, horn herbs, horn pill, Levitra, licorice, love dust, Love Potion No. 9, love potions, MDMA (Ecstasy), mandrake, mango, medina, oysters, poke, poppers, prolonger, quince, relics, rhino horn, sarsaparilla, sexual aids, snappers, Spanish Fly, Special K (Ketamine, a veterinary tranquillizer), Viagra, X (Ecstasy), yohimbine

Spanish Fly: made from the wings of the Cantharis Vesicatoria beetle. When ingested, it irritates the urethra so people have sex to relieve the severe genital itching.
Aroma, aroma of man, Butyl, disc cleaner, poppers, and snappers: all are synonyms for Amyl Nitrate.
Mango: consumption of this fruit is said to improve the taste of one's pussy.

Aroused (Male/Female)

SEE ALSO LUST, PROMISCUOUS, WET

Not surprisingly, many terms for sexual excitement refer to heat, fever, sweat.

accensus libidine, affy, amative, appetent, bar-on, begging for it, being a mongrel, being mustard, bent up, bitch-in-heat, blob on, boy crazy, blotty, brimming, bringing on, bulling, cagey, chucking a spread, chucked, cock happy, cockish, cocksmitten, concupiscent,

Blue balls: refers to the painful testicular congestion of blood in a man who is aroused but does not ejaculate. Synonymous with sexual frustration.
DSB: suffering from "deadly sperm build-up."

cracking a fat, creamy, cunt-itch, cunt struck, DSB, donkified, dripping, dripping for it, dripping pre-cum, engorged, expanding, exploding, fat, feeling fuzzy, feeling gay, feeling hairy, feeling the power of the pussy, fired up, fizzling at the bunghole, flavourful, foaming at the gash, fresh, frisky, fruity, fuckish, fuckstrated, full hard, full of fuck, full of gism, full on, fussed up, gagging for it, gamy/gamey, getting the hots for, getting juiced up, girl-crazy, girl-hungry, girl-mad, go letching after, goatish, hairy, hard up, having blueballs, having a bone-on, having a hard-on, having a pash for, having hot nuts, having hot rocks, having an itch, having an itch in the belly, having itchy feet, having itchy pants, having lover's balls, having peas in the pot, having the hots for, hawking your meat, hawking your mutton, honked, horizontally accessible, horn mad, horning, horny, horny as a rhino, hot, hot and bothered, hot as a firecracker, hot back(ed), hot for, hot in the biscuit, hot stuff, hot to trot, hot-assed, hot-blooded, hotpants, hungry, hunky, in a lather, in heat, in lust, in season, in the heat, in the mood, insatiable, intemperant, invading, jiggy, juicy, jungle fever, keen, lathered up, lecherous, leching, lewd, libidinous, licentious, lickerish, liquorous, lovey-dovey, lubricious, lust proud, lusty, magnificently stiff, man-hungry, manish, maris appentens, mashed, menacing, mettled, mushy, NDL, norwich, now hard, obviously aching, on for your greens, on heat, on the con, on the make, on the prowl, on the pull, oncoming, oozing, pulsating, prickstruck, primed, proud, pruny, prurient, purse proud,

Horny: derives from horn, *suggesting the erect penis but now used to describe libidinous women as well as men.*
Hot as a firecracker: a Canadian phrase first used in the 1920s.

raging hard-on, raising one, raking, rammish, rammy, ramstudious, randy, randy as a bitch in heat, randy as a drover's dog, randy as a mallee bull, randy as a three-legged grasshopper, randy-assed, ranting, raunchy, ready to rut, red combed, reddening, rehardened, rising boner, roaring hard, rock-hard ready, rollicky, rooty, ruttish, rutty,

Lecherous: from lecher, *the French word for* lick.
NDL: " nipples don't lie."
Randy: late 19th-century British; from ran-den, *which meant carousing or party-ing.*

salty, semi-flaccid, sexed up, smegma-leaking, softening, sperm-spewing, steamed up, straining, still hard, stomach thumping, suffering from lackanookie, suffering from night starvation, sweaty, switched on, syrupy, throbbing, ticklish, tingling, titty hardon (to have a), touchable, tumbling ripe, turned on, turning her on, twitching, venereal, wanton, weak in the knees, wet for, wide-on, willing, wired up, with it in your hand, worked up, yummy in the tummy

Aroused (to Throb)

SEE ALSO ERECTION
Bob, jerk, pound, pulsate, pulse, stroke, thud, thump, vibrate

Aroused (to Tremble)

convulse, flap, flicker, flutter, jerk, quake, quiver, shake, shim-mer, shiver, shudder, stagger, swag, totter, tremor, twitter, vibrate, wobble

Quiver: from the Old English term quiveren.

Aroused (Female)

SEE ALSO VAGINAL SECRETIONS
Wet and its adjectives commonly refer to vaginal lubrication and desire.
Beady, buttered-up, creamy, cummy, damp, dewy, drenched, dribbling, dripping, exuding, fluffy, foamy, frothy, glistening, glistening wet, gloppy, gooey, greasy, juicy, lathered, leaking, lubed, lubricated, luscious, lustrous, milky, moist, moistened, oily, oozing, oozy, ready, secreting, seeping, sleek, slick, slimy,

slippery, smeared, soaked, soaking, soapy, sodden, sopping, spilling, sweaty, tomcat, trickling, wet

Asshole: SEE ANUS

Attractive (Female) (Adjectives)
SEE ALSO HANDSOME (MALE)

In the 1970s, the influence of second-wave feminism in the lesbian community meant that gay women were thinking critically about the objectification of women, and consequently, were careful not to objectify one another. More recently, third-wave feminism and queer theory, both highly focussed on the linguistic power of "taking back" words, have become more influential, and many lesbian-specific and reappropriated terms are coming into use.

PHOTO: DIANNE WHELAN

Against the law, all that, alluring, approachable, attractive, awesome, babelicious, beautiful, beddable, bedroom eyes (has), bedworthy, best-built, bitcher, bitchin', bitching, blazing, bodacious, boobalicious, built, built for comfort, busty, buxom, choice, cute, curvy, dishy, doable, doe-like, doll, dreamy, drooly, easy on the eyes, enticing, Eve-like, eye candy, fetching, fine, finie, fit, fly, foxy, fuckable, georgeous, ginchy, glam, gnarly, handsome, has bedroom eyes, has pulling power, has sex appeal, haveable, heartbreakin', hot, hotcha, hugsome, hunky, looks like a million bucks, mobile, neat, Nice Lady, oochie, oomphy, oughta be a law, pretty, punchable, purty, radiant,

Stacked: the recent theorizing of femme as an independent gender expression has lead to a resurgence of many pulpy adjectives, i.e.: glam, foxy, lovely.
Buxom: fat activists like Nomy Lamm and Beth Ditto challenge the sizist leanings of the queer community by presenting sexually confident personas and choosing to celebrate their curves when they describe themselves. Also: buxom, curvy, busty.

red hot, right on time, rompworthy, sexational, sexy, shaggable, sizzlin', smashing, smokin', snappy, snazzy, stacked, stacks up nice, statuesque, stunning, such a mona, sweet,table grade, tasty, tight, to-die-for, twisty

VGL: very good looking

Balls: SEE TESTICLES

Bear
Developed in the late 1980s and early 1990s, bear culture composed of hirsute (both body and face) gay men, ususally physically larger than average.
arb, acrctophile, bear chaser, Bear Code, behr (moustache only), black bear, bruin, grizzly, hirsute, husbear, huscub, Koala (blonde fur), leather bear, male bear, muscle bear, otter, polar bear (greying), ursophile, wolf, woof

Bear Code: a bear version of the Kinsey Scale rating one's "beariness" by their amount of body and facial hair.
Black bear: an African-American bear.
Bruin: A bear who plays sports.
Husbear/ huscub: a bear boyfriend or husband.
Otter: a skinny man who is into bears.
Wolf: an older bear who prefers younger men, a.k.a. pups. Or an aggressive Otter.
Woof: bear slang for hot man or go, girl!

Bedroom
Not the queerest place for sex but it will do, in a pinch.
bedchamber, boudoir, chamber, cradle, crib, cubicle, doss, dungeon, fuck pit, guest room, hotbed, letting, pad, pit, playroom, shag pad
Boudoir: from the French bouder, *meaning to pout (as in a place to pout).*
> *I am being led and*
> *I am being led*
> *I am being led gently to bed*
> *—Gertrude Stein*

Bisexual

Even in the gay community, many terms for bisexual suggest either sexual confusion or treachery, reflecting persistent negative attitudes towards individuals who refuse to "pick a side."

> *Bisexuality immediately doubles your chances for a date on a Saturday night.*
> —Woody Allen

AC/DC, ambidextrous, ambiguous, ambisextrous, ambisexual, amphigenous inversion, amphisexual, Androgynophylia, batting and bowling, batting for both teams, betty bothways, bi, bi-curious, bi-kinky, bi-possible, bibi, bi-chick, bi-guy, bicoastal, bisexuous, BSO, bungie boy, butcher boy, byke,

Amphisexual: from the Latin amphi for on both sides.
BSO: "Bi significant other."
Butcher boy: a gay man who has sex with a lesbian.
Bungie boy/girl: reference to bungie jumping, an "extreme sport" involving jumping from great heights, attached by a bungie cord.
Byke: a bisexual dyke
CK1: hipster talk for somebody "bi," referring to a Calvin Klein perfume.

CK1, confused, convertible, door's ajar, double adapter, double gaited, double life man, drinks from both taps, Dyke tester, fence-fucker, flexual, flip, flip-flop, fruit-picker, gate-swinger, Gillette blade, gray cat,

Door's ajar: noun for one whose imminent coming out has been predicted.
Fence-fucker: derives from sitting on the fence, which suggests indecisiveness.
Flexual: open to same sex activity without identifying as gay.

greedy, half-and-half, half-bent, half rice half chips, happy shopper, heteroflexible, Horatian, intermediate, jack of all trades, jack of both sides, Jo-Ann, kiki, licks both sides of the stamp, mercenary, neither Arthur nor Martha, omnisexual, plays for both teams, plugs in both ways, questioning, rides a Bi-cycle, rides side-saddle, sexoschizia, sexually confused, shops on both sides of the street, side-saddle queen, simulsexual, swings both ways, switch hitter, TBH, try-sexual, twixter, two-way baby, two-way Johnny, versatile, waffler, wears bi-focals, yo-yo

TBH: "to be had."
Try-sexual: tries anything.
Switch hitter: 20th-century American term; derives from baseball terminology for an ambidextrous hitter.

Bite/Biting

SEE ALSO KISS, LICK, SWALLOW
chew, chomp, chow down, eat, hickey, love bite, mark up, munch, nab at, nibble, nip, odaxelagnia, pierce, sample, snack, taste, teeth marks, wound

Odaxelagnia: from the Greek, meaning arousal from biting.

Blow Job: SEE FELLATIO

Bottom/Top: SEE FETISH, SODOMY

Boyfriend

SEE ALSO LOVER
admirer, ace lane, adventure, back-door man, beau, beaufriend, bedfellow, best fellow, better half, bf, boo, boy toy, boyf, bread-winner, brown bagger, bones (the), buffalo, biscuit roller, companion, constant companion, daddy, domestic partner, fancy man, friend, goonie, GSO, his lordship, honey man, hubbie/hubby, item, jellyroll, john, just good friends, king, lad, life partner, longtime companion, lover, main man, male friend, man, man friend, man of my dreams/MOMD, mate, mister, monkey man, Mr. Right, mule, my guy, O and O, old man, old pot, opp, other half, pa, papa gâteau, Papa Noel, partner, patron,

petit ami, pilaf, playmate, PNB, pot and pan, protector, romance, roommate, Santa Claus, shack man, significant other, sigot /sother, spouse, steady, sugar daddy, sweet daddy, sweet man, sweet papa, sweetback, third party, toy boy, umfriend, weekend man, wife

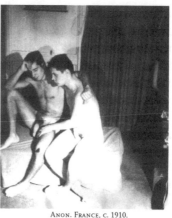

ANON. FRANCE, C. 1910.
THOMAS WAUGH COLLECTION

GSO: "gay significant other."
MOMD: "man of my dreams."
O and O: "one and only."
Pilaf: "person I'm loving and fucking."
PNB: "potential new boyfriend."
Sigot/sother: significant other.
SOD: "sleepover date."
Sugar daddy: suggests a wealthy, generous boyfriend. Similar terms include sugar and honey, goldmine, money-honey, *and* oyster.
Umfriend: what you call your boyfriend when you're not ready to out yourself (i.e., "he's my, um ... friend").

Breasts

SEE ALSO NIPPLES, CHEST

Historically, most slang terms for breasts have been invented by heterosexual men whose use of both idealizing metaphor and derogation boggles the mind. Increasingly, women have created their own pet names.

Breast synonyms win third prize for sheer numbers after penis *and* copulation.

apple dumplings, apples, appurtenances, B-cups, babaloos, babooms, baby bar (the), baby pillows, bag(s), balcony, balloon(s), baloobas, baps, barbettes, Barnes & Noble, bazongas, bazonkers, bazoom(s), bazoomas, bazoongies, bazumbas, beach bars, beanbags, beauties, beautiful chest, beautiful pair, beaver-tails, begonias, bell peppers, bellys, berks, berthas, best friends, bettys, bezongas, big brown eyes, bikini fillers, bikini stuffers, bings, birds, blatters, blobs, blossoms, blubbers, bobbers, Bobsey Twins, body, bon bons, bongos, boobies, boobifers, boobs, boobulars, booby, boom booms, borsties, boosiasms, bosom(s), boulders, bouncers, bra-buster(s), brace and bits, brassiere food, breastworks, Bristol bits,  Bristol City/Cities, Bristols, BSH, bubbies, bubbles, bubs, buckets, buddies, buds, buffers, bulbs, bumpers, bumpies, bumps, bust(s), butter-bags, butter-boxes, buzwams, c-cups, cajooblies, cakes, cans,

Boobs: from bubs, *an Elizabethan term for breasts. Bub also meant* drink.
Bristol Cities: rhymes with titties.
BSH: "British standard handfuls."

cantaloupes, casabas, cat heads, cat(s) and kitties, Charlies, charms, chee-chees, cherries, chestal area, chest, chestnuts, chichis, chichitas, chubbies, chussies, cleavage, cliff, coconuts, cokernuts, cooters, couple, cream jugs, croopers, cupcakes, cups, D-cups,

Many breast terms refer to lactation: i.e., cream jugs, milkers, milk jugs.

dairies, dairy, dairy farm, diddies, diddles, digs, din-dins, dinner, double D-cups, draggy udders, dried-up titties, droopers, dubbies, dugs, dumpling shop, dumplings, dzwony, Easts and Wests, Euter, eyes, fainting fits, falsies, fat sacks, fatty breasts, feeding bottles, figure, flab hangings, flabby melons, flapjacks, flip-flaps, flip-flops, floppers, floppy tits, floppy whites, flops, foofs, fore-buttocks, fountain, fried eggs, front, front door,

Gay deceivers: falsies.
Gib tesurbs: an approximate backward phrase for big breasts.

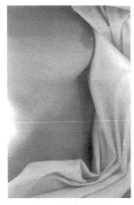

PHOTO: DIANNE WHELAN

front parlour, frontage, fuckin' tits, fun bags, garbonzos, gay deceivers, gazongas, gentleman's pleasure, gib tesurbs, girls (the), glands, globes, goonas, gourds, grapefruits, grapes, groodies, growths, guavas, gubbs, hairy stubs, hammertons, hand-warmers, hands, hangers, hanging tits, headlights, heavers, hemispheres, hog jaws, hogans, honeydew melons, honeydews, honkers, hoofers, hooters, itty bitty titty/ies, jamboree bags, jellies, jellyfish, jelly-on-springs, Jersey cities, jiggle bosoms, jobbies, jubbies, jubes, jublies, jugs, juicy peaches, jujubes, kajoobies, kahunas, kettle-drums, knackers, knobs, knockers, lactoids, lemons, Lewis & Witties, loaves, lollies, lollos, love blobs, love bubbles, love buds, love pillows, lumps, lung nuts, lung warts, lungs, Mae Wests,

Mae Wests: refers to the well-known bosomy camp actress, but also rhymes with breasts.

magafi, mammaries, mammary glands, mammets, mams, Manchesters, mangoes, maracas, marshmallows, Mary Poppins, masob(s), massive mammaries, mazoomas, meat, meatballs, melons, memories, mezoomas, milk-bottles, milk-buckets, milk-glands, milk-jugs, milk-sacks, milk-shop, milk-walk, milkers, milkshakes, Milky Way (the), mole hills, mollicoes, mollies, moon balloons, mosquito bites, mounds, mount of lilies, mountains, muffins, murphies, nangles, nature's fonts, nay-nays, niblets, nice handful, nice puppies,

Not surprsingly food-related sexual slang is well-represented in the breast category: apples, coconuts, grapes, grapefruits, honeydew melons, oranges, peaches, lemons, watermelons.

nice set, nick nacks, ninnies, ninny-jugs, nipple leather, no tits, norgies, norks, Norma Snockers, nubbies, nubs, nuggets, old saggy tits, oojahs, oomlaters, oranges, orbs, other parts, pair, pancakes, panters, pantry shelves, papayas, paps, peaches, peanuts, pears, pechitos, pellets, person (the), personalities, pimentos fritos, pimples, playground (the), poonts, porcelain spheres, potatoes, pretty lungs, pumpkins, pumps, pus glands, rack, ree-langers, rib cushions, rising beauties, rocks, sacks, sagging summer squash, saggy pig tits, scar-crossed prunes, scones,

semiglobes, set of jugs, shirt potatoes, shit bags, shock absorbers, skin, slugs, snorbs, soft cadaby, squashy bits, spooters, stack(ed), stonkers, superdroopers, sweat glands, sweater meat, sweater treats, sweet rolls, sweetest valley, swingers, T&A, Tale of Two Cities, tamales, tatas, teacups, teats, tetinas, tetitas, them, thousand pities, threepenny bits, tired old tits, tiskies, tits, titties, titty, tomatoes, tnt, tonsils, top, top 'uns, top bollocks, top buttocks, top ones, top set, top-heavy, topballocks, topless, toraloorals, torpedo(s), towns and cities,

T&A: "tits and ass."
TNT: "two nifty tits."
Willets: Polari for breasts.

tracy bits, treasure, treasure chest (the), tremblers, trey bits, tube-socks with a golf ball, turkeys, twin lovelies, twins (the), udders (the), ugly fat knockers, ugly jugs, upper deck (the), upper works (the), veiled twins, vital statistics, voos, wallopies, walnuts, wammers, wards, warmest valley (the), warts, waterbags, watermelons, whammers, white flowers, whites, willets, wrinkled tits, yams, yoinkahs

Brothel, Male

SEE GAY SEX VENUES

Essayist and gay historian Rictor Norton remarks that the emergence of terms for male brothels and homosexuality in the early 18th century is related to the increase in survelliance and establishment of organized police forces.

Benny house, birdcage, boy's smoking house, bullring camp, call house, carsey, cock shop, crystal palace, flowershop, jag house, knishery, massage parlour, molly house, peg house, sauna club, sauna parlour, service station, show house, snake ranch, spintry, strip joint

ANON. FRANCE, C. 1910.
THOMAS WAUGH COLLECTION

Knishery: American-Yiddish term for brothel referencing the meat-filled pastries.

Butch

The word butch is used by gay men and lesbians but has different meanings depending on the user and the subject. In a queer context, butch refers to a person or behaviour that presents as hyper-masculine. A woman who reads as butch reveals her queerness, whereas a man described as butch may be trying to conceal his queerness.

Ape, baby butch, b-girl, blood, boi, bull, bullish, bull-dyke, butch daddy, caveman, chapstick lesbian, fagdyke, hard butch, he-man, honcho, jock, manly,
Fagdyke: A butch who has sex with other butches.

mannish, masculine, mascularious, nail, rough, tough, tuff guy, soft butch, stone butch, "straight acting", stud, tuff guy, ultra-butch, virile, wears boxer shorts

Buttocks

SEE ALSO ANUS

The buttocks, though among the largest muscles in the human body, are systematically ignored as entries in standard thesauri.

Ass is an American derivation of the Old English slang word ass (for buttocks).
Arse is the term used in the U.K.

achers, acre, after part, ampersand, anatomy, archer, arm cheeks, arse ass, assteriors, BA, back, back parts, backland, backside, backway, balcony, basement, batti, beam, beautocks, behind, bim, bippy, biscuits, blind cupid, blot, bogy, bom, bombosity,

BA: "bare ass."
"Baby Got Back" was a number 1 hit for Sir Mix-A-Lot in 1992.

bomsey, boo-boo, boody, bootie, booty, bosom of the pants, bottle and glass, bottom, botty, breech, broad beam, bubble butt, bucket, bum, bumbo, bummy, bump, bumper kit, bunchy, buns, buns aplenty, butt, butter, caboose, cake, camera obscura, can, canister set,

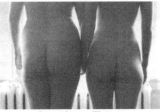

PHOTO: DIANNE WHELAN

catastrophe, cheeks, chips, chuff, clunes, cooler, corybungus, croup, crumpet, crupper, cul, culo, cupcakes, daily mail, date, derriere, differential, dinger, dish, dock, dokus, double jug, double juggs, drop, duff, dummock, duster, Dutch dumplings, English muffins, fanny, fat ass,

Bubble butt: modern-day American term for a perfectly rounded ass.
Bum: Middle English term for buttocks; from the Dutch bom.
Corybungus: Polari for butt.
Daily mail: rhymes with tail.

fife and drum, flankey, flanks, fleshy part of the thigh, fud, fun, fundament, fundamental features, fundillo, gazeet, gazonga, gazooney, gluteal region, glutes, gluteus maximus, gluton, Greek side (the), hams, handlebars of love, hangover, hard-ass, haunch, haunches, heinie, hind, hind end, hinder end, hinder parts, hindside, hinterland, honey rolls, hootenanny, Hugh Jass, hunkers, jacksy pardy, jeer, jibs, jubilee, juff, jutland, kabedis, kazoo,

keel, keester, keister, la-la, labon-
za, lard ass, latter end, limb, little
Mary, luds, male tail, meat pillows, moon, mottob, mudflaps,

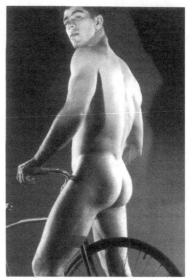

Heinie: 20th-century American term for
hind end.
Glutes: jock abbreviation for gluteus, *from
the Greek* gloutos *for* buttock.
*Jacksy: a contemporary British slang term
for* anus.
*Mottob: an example of slang derived from
backward spelling.*

nachas, nates, nockandro, North
Pole, oil bags, paddies, parking
place, parts behind, pod, poop,
pooper, posteriors, postern, prat,
prats, pressed ham, promonto-

BRUCE OF LOS ANGELES, U.S., c. 1960.
THOMAS WAUGH COLLECTION

ries, quoit, rass, rear, rear end, rosey, rounders, royal buns, rum,
rumble seat, rumdadum, rump, rumpus, rumpus delecti, rusty
dusty, saddle leather, scut, seat, seat of the pants, sess, set of
pairs, sit-me-down, sit-upon, sitter, sitting room, smallers, sot-
ting, south end, speedo boy, spread, squatter, stern, sugar cookies, Sunday face, tail, toby, tocks, tokus, toosh, tooshie, toute,
tuches, tushie, twin bills, under-arm, underside, yeastful

Tokus (also tochas, tockus): from Yiddish for buttocks.
Yeastful: an oblique reference to buns.
To expose your buttocks: do a moon job; flash your butt/bum; hang a moon;
moon; red eye.

Caress

SEE ALSO FONDLE, KISS
bear-hug, belly-crunch, bill, cajole, canoodle, clasp, cling, clutch,
cock pluck, coo, court, court and spark, cradle, cuddle, dally,

JOHN BARRINGTON, U.K., c. 1940's
THOMAS WAUGH COLLECTION

dinkydiddle, draw close, embrace, get physical, goose, grope, guzzle, hold, huddle, hug, lovey-dovey, lumber, make love, make love to, peck and neck, rock, slake, slap and tickle, soothe, spoon, squeeze, stroke, take into your arms, tickle, touch

Spoon: dates back to the 19th century; suggested both foreplay and affectionate touching. In modern-day usage, refers to two people embracing while facing the same direction, as in bed.

Casual Sex Partner/One-Night Stand

Alley affair, alley queen, fling, fuck buddy, oncer, onetimer

Cheat on (to)

SEE ALSO PROMISCUOUS, MONOGAMY

burn, cat around, chippy on, chibby chase, cruise, dilly-dally, dog on, double-cross, engage in an extra-marital affair, engage in extracurricular activities, fan your ass, fan your pussy, fish, flag, flirt, fool around, give up rhythm, go on a fishing expedition,

Philander: from the Greek philandros, meaning loving men.
Vampire: a gay man who steals others' partners.

hit and run, horse around, jack around, jazz around, monkey about, perv about, philander, play around, play checkers, play games with, play the field, player (to be a), put horns on, put it about, shoot the thrill, step out on, tease, tomcat, trick out, two-time, vampire

Chest (Male)

SEE ALSO MUSCULAR, BREASTS, NIPPLES

A muscular male chest is a new Western aesthetic preoccupation. Many new terms

will likely emerge as gay men renew their memberships at the Cult of Fitness.

Bitch-tits, boy-breast, boy-boobs, breast, brisket, disco tits, epilation mountains, gym tits, pecky, pecoramas, pecs, pecs for days, pectorals, ribs, thorax, tit freak/queen, tits, tittier, torso, upper trunk

KRIS STUDIO, C. 1960.
THOMAS WAUGH COLLECTION

Bitch tits: gynecomastia caused by steroid use.
Pecky: refers to a guy with big pecs.
Tit freak/queen: a gay man with a fetish for the male chest.

Clitoris

SEE ALSO GENITALIA, LABIA, VAGINA

The precise etymological origin of this term is unclear. Greek words for hill, famous, *and* hidden *have been suggested.*

beetle's bonnet, bell, boy in the boat, budgie's tongue, button, clit, clitty, clown's hat, dat, dot, fun button, girl cock/dick, goal-keeper, jewel terrace, jointess, joy buzzer, laborator natural, little guy, little man, little man in the boat, little ploughman, little shame tongue, love bud, love button, love dart, membrum muliebre, nuts, pearl, praline, prawn of pleasure, sensitive spot, spare tongue, slit, slit bit, sugared diamond, taste bud

Boy in the boat: a British term from the 1800s, the boat being the vulva.
Girl cock/dick: a term used in lesbian porn.
Jewel terrace: a poetical term from the Chinese.

Closet Case

The closet is the central euphemistic term to articulate our homophobic culture's urge to police and hide queer culture. (See Eve Sedgewick, The Epistemology of the Closet).

Abigail, angel with a dirty face, beard, BMQ, bi-curious, bunker shy, canned fruit, closet case/CC, closet queen, closet queer, con-fused, crushed fruit, dash, discrete, "don't ask, don't tell," fake

room, flinker, front marriage,

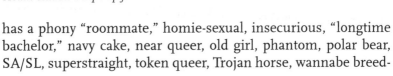

*Beard: a woman who is used by a gay man to show that he is
"straight."*
BMQ: black market queer.
Don't ask, don't tell: policy of the U.S. armed forces, revised under   J. Edgar Hoover
President Clinton, regarding gays in the military.
Front marriage: a gay man and a lesbian married to each other to hide their sexuality.
Homie-sexual: a hip-hop fan who's in the closet.

has a phony "roommate," homie-sexual, insecurious, "longtime
bachelor," navy cake, near queer, old girl, phantom, polar bear,
SA/SL, superstraight, token queer, Trojan horse, wannabe breeder

Navy cake: a gay sailor.
SA/SL: "straight-acting/ straight looking."
Superstraight: one who compensates for homosexual urges by becoming ultra-heterosexual in behaviour.

Cocksucker: SEE FELLATIO, ONE WHO PERFORMS

Come: SEE EJACULATE (TO), ORGASM, SEMEN

Come Out of the Closet (to)
SEE ALSO GAY MALE, HOMOSEXUALITY, GAY (TO HIDE YOUR
HOMOSEXUALITY)

IN SAN FRANCISCO IN
1977, HARVEY MILK
BECAME THE US'S FIRST
OPENLY GAY ELECTED OFFI-
CIAL.

Terms for revealing gay or lesbian sexual identity are surprisingly few despite the fact that coming out is an increasingly common practice in Western society.
accept your sexuality, be brought out, come
clean, declare, debut, fly the rainbow flag, discover your gender, drop a feather, drop your
beads, drop your hairpins, fly the rainbow flag,
go over, jump out (with both feet), jump out of
the closet,

Until you are out, you won't know what happiness is.
—Sir Ian McKellen, actor

lay it out, learn a new way, let your hair down, on the turn, out (to), reveal your homosexuality, show your true colours, tell the folks, turn the corner, unpin your back hair (to), wave the rainbow, wear your badge

PHOTO: DIANNE WHELAN

Out (to): when a closeted celebrity is publicly revealed to be gay without their consent.

Condom

SEE ALSO CONTRACEPTION

The oldest illustration of a condom was found in Egypt and dates back more than 3,000 years. An early modern prophylactic may have been invented by a physician, a Dr. Condom, to protect his sovereign, King Charles II (1630-1685). Alternate stories suggest that Condom was a colonel in the British military.

American sock, armour, BB, B.C., bag, baggie, balloon, bishop, blob, body stocking, bone balloon, boner bag,

BB: "barebacking."
B.C.: "before condoms."

"For the first time I did engage in armour, which I found but dull satisfaction."
—James Boswell, journal entry, 1763

bubble-gum machine, cadet, candy wrapper, cap, cassock, cling film, coat, cock sock, condom machine, condominium, Coney Island whitefish, cootie catcher, crum drum, cundum, diving bell, diving suit, dome, double bag, dubs, Durex, envelope, flunkey, flute mute, Fourex, franger, French letter, French tickler, frenchie/frenchy, frog, froggie, frogskin, fuck rubber, Glad bag/wrap, glove, hard hat, head gasket, headliner, jim, jimmy, jimmy hat, jit bag, jism jacket, jo-bag, johnny, jolly bag, joy bag, joy sock, knob sox, latex, latex love, lettre Anglaise, life jacket, life preserver, life saver, love envelope, love glove, lubie (lubricated),

Historically the French referred to a condom as une lettre Anglaise *and the English called it a* French letter.
Latex love: sex with a condom.
Love envelope: 1980s U.S. gayspeak for a condom.
Rubber up: to put on a condom.

Manhattan eel, Mr. Happy's business suit, muffler, muzzle, nightcap, noddy, overcoat, party hat, party pack, pecker pack, plumber's helper, plumbing fixture, Port Said garter, propho, prophylactic, protection, raincoat, ribbed condom, rough rider (ribbed), rozzer, rubber, rubber boot, rubber duck, rubber duckie, rubber johnny, rubber pill, rubber sock, rubber up, sack, safe, scum sack, scumbag, shag bag, sheath, Shiek, shower-cap, skin, sleeve, slicker, snake skin, sock, squeegee, stiffy stocking, stopcock, stopper tube, suddle, sweater, tickler, tool bag, washer, wetsuit, Wiener wrap, willy-welly

Ride bareback: vaginal or anal sex without a condom.
Showering in a raincoat: sex with a condom.
The invention of an increasing number of terms for condom is an AIDS-era phenomenon.

Crotch (Male)
SEE ALSO GENITALIA, MALE

Angry Inch, basket, basketeer, bulge, bump, hump, jewel case, laundry, lunch, meat basket, mound, package, packet, snack-pack, the goods, yummies,

Basketeer: someone who stares at male crotches.

"My sex change operation got botched,
my guardian angel fell asleep on the watch,
now all I've got is a Barbie Doll crotch, I've got an Angry Inch"
—Hedwig (John Cameron Mitchell)
singing in Hedwig and the Angry Inch

Cruise (to)

bait, basket shop, bat your eyes at, break your neck, bumchat, catch, chase, check out, cheese (to), Christmas carolling, circle the circus, clock (to),

Break your neck: do a double take to cruise a hottie.
Christmas carolling: checking out all the new glory holes.
Circle the circus: refers to Picadilly circus, a popular London cruising area.

come on to, convince, court, crack on, do a 180-degrees, do a 360-degrees, eye, eye contact (to make), eyeball, eye-fuck, fish, flam, follow, fish, game (to), gawk, gay gaze, gaydar (to use my), git wit, flash on, get, get a load of, get busy, get to home plate, give a come-hither look, give a double "O," give one the cyclops, give the glad eye, give the once over, give the reckless eyeball, go after, go basket shopping, go for, grill (to), have eye sex, hawk, hit on, hoof (to),

Dykedar/gaydar: intuition for detecting other gays and lesbians.
Hoof: on the prowl.
Ping: the trans term for detecting other transfolk.

hold the glims on, jeff, jock (to), lamp, look over, look up and down at, lumber, make bedroom eyes at, make goo goo eyes at, make a dead set for, make a pass at, make a play for, make moves on, mousetrap, move in on, nail, not take no for an answer, ogle, on a meat safari, on bush patrol, on the bridge, on the pull, on

the make, on the pirate (be), on the peep, perve, ping, prop up, pull, persist, play canasta, play musical chairs, power-cruise, prowl, pull a quick park, push upon, put the hard word on, put the moves on, put the rush on, reel in, rope in, rubberneck (to), scam, scope, scope the local units, score, scout,

scrutinize, seduce, see, sleuth (to), stalk, size up, spot, spy, stare (at), strain your eyes, strain your neck, sticky eye contact, suck in, sweep off your feet, sweet-talk, tailgate, take a dekko, take a look at, take in, take notice of, track with, troll, trot, view, watch over, whore laps (do), zoom

Whore laps: to circle the bar for quick love.
"Who's Zoomin' Who?" was a hit for Aretha Franklin in 1985.

Cunnilingus

SEE ALSO ORAL SEX

From the Latin cunnus *(vulva) and* lingere *(to lick).*

barking at the ape, bird washing, box lunch, canyon yodeling, clam lapping, clitorilingus, cunning linguist (be a), cunt lapping, doormat bashing, drink at the fuzzy cup, eating out, eating pussy, egg McMuff, face job, fanny noshing, French, French tricks, French way, fress, go downstairs for breakfast, gorilla in the washing machine, growl at the badger, hammer tongue, have a moustache, head, larking, kiss it down, lick-twat, lickety-split, lip work, lunch at the lazy Y, muff barking, muff diving, ocean pinking, pug noshing, red wings, sack lunch, scalp, sip at the fuzzy cup, sixty-nine, skin diving, skull job, skulling, smoking the fur, splitting n hitting, soixante-neuf, sucking cunt, swap spit, tongue bath, tongue fucking, tongue job, tuna taco, vice versa, whistling in the dark

Soixante-neuf/sixty-nine: dates to the 19th century in France and refers to mutual oral sex as visually suggested by the number itself.

Cunnilingus (to Perform)

blow some tunes, brush your teeth, carpet munch, clam dive, clean the cage out, clean up the kitchen, dental dam (use a), dine at the Y, dip in the bush, dive, dive a muff, dive in the canyon, drink at the fuzzy cup, eat, eat a tuna sandwich, eat a tuna taco, eat at the Y, eat hair pie, eat out, eat pussy, eat seafood, eat sushi, face the nation, give a blow job, give head, go boating, go down on, go under the house, go way down South in Dixie, grin in the canyon, growl at the badger, have a moustache, have a tuna sandwich, impersonate Stalin, lap cunt, lick-a-chick, make mouth music, muff dive, mumble in the moss,

Dental dam: a latex barrier used during cunnilingus to reduce the risk of transmission of STDs.
Muff diving: a 20th-century American euphemism, though muff dates to the 17th century, drawing parallels between the female genitals and a furry hand warmer.

munch, munch the bearded clam, punch in the mouth, queening, scalp, sip at the fuzzy cup, sit on your face, skin dive, sneeze in the basket, sneeze in the cabbage, sneeze in the canyon, suck, talk to the canoe driver, telephone the stomach, tongue, tongue fuck, whistle in the weeds, yodel, yodel in the canyon (of love), yodel in the gully, yodel up the valley

Queening: When a woman sits on a partner's face, forcing her genitalia into their nose and mouth.
Yodelling: a Swiss form of calling out involving vibration of the mouth, throat, and tongue, all of which enhance this particular sexual activity.

Cut: SEE PENIS, CIRCUMCISED, FORESKIN

Defecate (to)

SEE ALSO FETISHES, URINATE (TO)

accident (have an), Andy Capp, BM (bowel movement, have a), bury a quaker, capoop, cast, cast your pellet, choke a darkie, chuck a turd, clart, clear out, cramber, crap, cuck, deposit, dirty your pants, dispatch your cargo, do a dike, do a job, drop your load, drop your wax, drop turds, drop your ass, dump, ease nature, ease your bowels, evacuate the bowels, Edgar Britt, excused (be), fill your pants, foul (yourself), george, go, go to the bathroom, grunt, Irish shave, loosen the bowels, make a big hit, make a ca-ca, make a deposit, make a poo poo, make art, move your bowels, number two (do), pass a clot, perform the work of nature, pick a daisy, play hockey, poo, poop, post a letter, press a ham, press a shoelace, quat, relieve yourself, ride the porcelain bus, rump, scat action, scumber, shift, shit, siege, sit on the throne, smell the place up, soil, soil your linens, soil your pants, squat, stool (be at), take a crap, take a dump, take a poo, take a shit, unfeed, use paper, visit the potty, void

Crap: a 19th-century British term for feces, used here as a verb.

Desire (to)

SEE ALSO AROUSED, LOVE (TO)

Compare this list to verbs used for love and lust. As in real life, distinctions often blur.

ache for, be hot for, carry a torch for, covet, covetous of (be), crave, die for (to), dig, fall for someone, fancy, feel your oats, get one going, get your nose open, go for, gun for, hanker after, have a hard-on for, have a jones for, have a pash for, have a passion for, have an itch for, have chemistry, have eyes for, have/got it bad, have hot nuts for, have hot pants for, have your tongue hanging out for, have the hots for, honk for, hooked, hunger for, hurting for, in deep (be), in need of (be), itch for, keen about (be), keen on someone (be), languish

for/after, letch after, letch for, letch over, long for, lust after, mad on someone (be), moon for, miss, need, partial to (be), pine for, prime your pump, put lead in your pencil, set your heart on, smitten with (be), soft on (be), starved for (be), strong on, stuck on (be), taken with (be), thirst for, turned on (be), turned on by (be), wacky about (be), want, wish for, yearn for, yen for

Drag: SEE TRANSVESTITE

Dump (to): SEE END A RELATIONSHIP

Effeminate (Male)

SEE ALSO GAY MALE, ANDROGYNE

These mostly historical terms manage to degrade women and gender-atypical males in one fell swoop. For a critical analysis of modern psychiatry's view of effeminate boys, see Eve Sedgwick's essay, "How to Bring Your Kids Up Gay," in Fear of a Queer Planet, edited by Michael Warner.

ace-queen, Barbie, batty-man, beard flit, belle, Betty, bish, bitch, broken wrist, busy, buttercup, butterfly, camp, camp bitch, campy, cinderella, daffodil, daisy, delicate, dickless Tracey, double fruit, effete, effie, epicene, ethel, faggy, fairy, femme fatale, feminine, femme, femmy, flamboyant, flame(y), flamer, flaming, flit, flowery, foopy, fragile, fruitcake, fruity,

Double fruit: cute and queeny
Epicene: a grammatical term referring to nouns in Greek or Latin which can be either male or female and thus do not change form.
GAP: "gay American Princess."
Hesh: he-she.

GAP, girlish, girly, girly-mon, glittery, hasie, hen, hesh, huckle, lady-like, lah-de-dah, lacey, light-footed, light in the loafers, light on your feet, lilly-livered, limp, limp-wristed, lispy, loose in your loafers, macumeh/makomey/maku/manicou man, margery, Mary Ann, Mary, mincer, minty/mintee/mintie, Miss It, Miss

Photo: The New Congress

Nancy, Miss Thing, Molly Boy, moumoune, mouse, Nancy, Nelly, pansy, panty man, perthy, pixie, pood, poof, poofy, powder puff, prissy, pure silk, queeny, rabbit, royalie/royaly, screamer, screaming, screecher, "see Tarzan, hear Jane," sheena, shim, singed eyebrows (flaming), sissified, sissy, sissy boy, sissy pants, sissyish, soft sucker, sweet man, swish, swishy, tapette, tempermental, thithy, tunt, twiddlepoop, twinkle toes, Wendy, whoopsie, willy/willie, winny, womanish, womanly

Macumeh/makomey/maku/manicou man: West Indies term for an effeminate man.
Pood: a reference to pudding, i.e., wimpy.
"See Tarzan, hear Jane": a butch-looking man who sounds like a girl.
Nelly: Polari for effeminate.
Royalie/royaly: Australian term for effeminate and/or gay male.

"Camp is a homosexual sensibility with a soupçon of weariness"
—Ned Rorem, musician

Ejaculate (to)

SEE ALSO ERECTION, ORGASM, SEMEN

bibbing, blow a load, blow up, break, bust, bust a nut, bust out of the balls, bust your nuts, cheese, come up, crash your muck, climax, come, come off, come your cocoa, crash the yoghurt truck, cream, cum, die, discharge, do number three, drip (to), drop your load, ease yourself,

Bibbing: any preparation before sex that improves privacy, ie locking the door, or ease of clean up, i.e., using drop sheets or getting towels ready.
Come up: ejaculate during anal sex.
Do number three: refers to a third bodily discharge, numbers one and two being

urination and defecation.
Easter queen: a 1960s American term for a man who ejaculates prematurely.

Easter queen, effect emission, emit, empty the trash, erupt into a gulping throat, fill his ass, fill one with come, fill the throat, fire a shot, fire blanks, fire in the air, flood the throat, free the tadpoles, get a nut, get off, get your cookies off, get your nuts off, get your rocks off, get the upshoot, give your gravy, go, go off, gush, have an emission, have a little death,

Firing blanks: can refer to either a dry orgasm, or an orgasm by a man who has had a vasectomy.
Jiffy pop: premature ejaculation.
Little death: translated from the French une petite mort, *a literary allusion to orgasm used in the 1800s and 1900s.*

have a seminal emission, have a sexual reflex, have a spasm, have a sperm attack, have a wet dream, hive it, hole, jet forth (to), jet your juice, jiffy pop, jis, jiz, juice, knock one out, let go, lose your mess, melt, milk, monk, ooze, P.E., pee white, piss your tallow, pitch (to), play the whale, pop a nut, pop your cookies, pop your nuts, Quentin Quickfire, ranch, reach the big O, release, send out the troops, shoot, shoot into, shoot off, shoot a  batch, shoot a cream, shoot a creamy load, shoot a load, shoot a roe, shoot a wad, shoot over the stubble, shoot white, soak the sheets, spend, spermatize, spew, spew like a geyser, spill, splatter, splooge, spooch, spooj, spray, sprouting, spurting, squirting, spunk, spur (to), squeeze up, throw up, upshoot, wet dream (to have a), whitewash

P.E.: "premature ejaculation."

Quentin Quickfire: a premature ejaculator.
Spunk: British term from the 1800s; referred to a man's courage as well as his ejaculate.
"To come," suggesting orgasm, may have been first used by William Shakespeare.

End a Relationship (to)

abandon, air, annul, blow off, break up, bust up, call it quits, chuck, Dear John letters, dedomicile, desert, ditch, do the frank, do the off, drop, drop the pilot, dump, eject, end it, flush, forsake, freeze, give someone their walking papers, give the air, give the brush off/to, give the California kiss-off, go awol, jilt, kiss off, kick to the curb, leave, let down, orphaned (to be), push away, reject, run off, run out on, separate, split up, STBX, take the train, throw out, throw over, tip, turf, unload, untie the knot, up and leave, walk, walkout, write a Dear John letter

Dear John letters: emerged in the armed forces during World War II to signify a soldier who receives a letter of rejection from his partner back home. Now used in the context of being dumped by a same-sex lover.
Give the California kiss-off: refers to the high incidence of divorce in the Golden State.
Orphaned: to be dumped.
STBX: "soon to be ex."

.

Erection

SEE ALSO AROUSED, EJACULATE, PENIS

Terms for erection reveal both the unabashed machismo and bragging so common to male-derived erotic slang.

Aaron's rod, ant-eater, Bacchus march, baloney, barker, basket, bayonet, bazooka, bed flute, big man on campus, big number, biological reaction, biological response, bit of hard, bit of snug, bit of stiff, blue steeler, bone (the), bone hard, bone-on, boner, boneronie, bonk-on, bulge, Captain Hard, Captain Standish, carnal stump, charge, chubby, cockstand, colin, concomitant of desire, concrete donkey, crack a fat, crimson crowbar, cucumber, dawn horn, diamond cutter, distending, divining rod, dobber, erected, erectio penis, full, fully-engorged, fully erect, gun, hard, hard as a rock, , hard-bit, hardening, hard-on, hard-up,

Colin: Polari for erection.
Dobber/lazy lob on: a weak erection.
Bed flute/dawn horn/tent pole: a morning erection.
Lurching: refers to an inopportune erection.

having it on, heat in the meat, horn (the), horn colic, hornification, horse's hand-brake, hugely erect, in full-fig, Irish toothache, inflamed, iron-hard, Jack, jack-in-the-box, knob-ache, lance in rest, lazy lob on, lengthening, lift up, limp, live wire, lob, lurching, Marquess of Lorn, marabon stork, matitudinal erection, morning hard-on, morning pride, morning wood, Mr. Priapus, muddy waters, nearly hard, old Adam, old Hornington, old Horny, on the

CLARENCE TRIPP. U.S., C. 1945.
THOMAS WAUGH COLLECTION

bonk, on the honk, on the stand, penile erection, penis in erectus, pink steel, piss fat, piss hard-on, piss proud, pitching a tent in your shorts, poker, pole, pong, priapism, priapus, prick, prick pride, pride of the morning, prigpas, prod, proud below the navel, pruney, putter, rager, rail, ramrod, reamer, rigid, rigid digit, rise, rise in your Levi's, roaring horn, roaring jack, rock hard, rock python, rod, rod of love, root, schwing,

Piss proud: refers to the erection a man gets in the morning, usually in response to a need to urinate.
Rock python: mid-20th-century British term suggesting a hard snake.

semi-erect, September morn, sequoia, shaft, spike, stable, staff, stalk, stand, stand-on, standard, standing member, steely dan, stem, stiff, stiff and stout, stiff as a board, stiff deity, stiff one, stiff prick, stiff stander, stiffie, stiffy, still, stone-hard, stonk, stonk-on, stonker, stork, Sunday best, swelling, swollen, temporary priapism, tent, tent pole, thickened, thumper, tilt in your kilt, toothache, touch-on, tube of meat, tumescence, turgid, ultra-hard, up, urgently erect, utterly rigid, virile member, virile reflex, weapon, wingert, wood, woody

"A stiff prick has no conscience."—20th-century quasi-feminist graffiti
"Is that a gun in your pocket or are you just glad to see me?"—Mae West

Fart: SEE FLATUS, TO PASS

Fellatio
SEE ALSO FELLATIO (TO PERFORM), FELLATIO (ONE WHO PERFORMS), ORAL SEX

Fellatio has been, in many historical contexts, considered an immoral and perverted act, legally included under the rubric of sodomy. For straight people, it can still be considered a fetish. Fellatio is from the Latin fellare, *to suck.*

ATTRIB. LATTIMER, U.S., 1940s.
THOMAS WAUGH COLLECTION

210, barries/baris, blow job/BJ, blue jay, buccal onanism, chewy, deep throat, dsl, face pussy, face-fucking, french job, French polishing, French tricks, French way, gamarouche, gammy, gob-job, gorp, head, head job, Hooverism, Horatio, hose job, job, knob job, knob shining, larro, lick meat, lipwork, lollypop (have a), lunch, mouth music, nob-a-job, O-levels, oral, oral job, oral service, oral sex, penilictus, penilingus, penisuction, pipe job, piston job, pricknic, punishment, scooby snack, sixty-nine, skull-buggery, skull fuck, skull pussy, soixante-neuf, sucking lips, sucky-fucky, titty-oggy, tongue fucking, top-drawer, vice versa, zipper sex

Hooverism: refers to the action of a Hoover vacuum.
Pricknic: 20th-century American term; a playful combination of prick and picnic.

44

Fellatio (One Who Performs)

SEE ALSO FELLATIO, FELLATIO (TO PERFORM), GAY MALE

barbecue, beejayable, blow monkey, blow-boy, bugle boy, c--r, cannibal, catch, cocksmoker, cocksucker, Dennis, dick sucker, dicky licker, face artist, fellator, flake, fluter, French artist, glut, glutton, goot gobbler, goat throat, gobbler, head worker, hose monster, icing expert, iron jaws, jaw queen, king expert, knob gobbler, language expert, lapper, lickbox, man-eater, mouth whore, mouth worker,

Beejayable: someone you'd like to give a blow job.
C---r (cocksucker): an example of how "bad words" were alluded to in print, but not spelled fully, as a way of avoiding obscenity charges. Also a derogatory term for a gay man.
Iron jaws: a particularly talented fellator.

muncher boy, nephew, nibbler, one who failed the gag reflex test, oral specialist, orchid eater, peter eater, peter puffer, philatelist, piccolo player, pick spigot, pink pants, pudlicker, punk, queen, receiver, sally, scumsucker, senor-eata, skin diver, smoker, spigot sucker, stand, sucker, suckster, vacuum cleaner

ANON. GERMANY, C. 1920s.
THOMAS WAUGH COLLECTION

Fellatio (to Perform)

SEE ALSO FELLATIO (ONE WHO PERFORMS)

auto-fellatio, bag, bagpipe, "bite me," bite your crank, blow, blow off, blow your skin flute, blow your whistle, blue jay (to), cannibalize, cap, cocksuck, cop a hot one, cuff your carrot, deep throat, dick (to), dick lick, do (to), eat, eat cock, eat your meat, feed your face, flip-flop, flute, french, get a facial, get down on your knees, give a dam, give cone, give head, gnosh, go to church (i.e., kneel and pray), go down on, gob the knob, gobble, gobble your goo, gobble your worm, gum, gunch, he-blow, hoover, inhale the oyster, job, jurry, lap, lay the lip, lick, lick dick, lick your prick, mug, munch, num, piccolo player, pipe (to clean), plate,

CLARENCE TRIPP, U.S., c. 1945.
THOMAS WAUGH COLLECTION

Auto-fellatio: refers to someone who can suck himself.
Get a facial: modern slang for being fellated, face cream also referring to semen.
Plate: Polari for fellate (to).

play your flute, play your horn, polish your knob, prick-lick, pull on some tubing, pull some peepee, receive holy communion, say high mass, scoff, serve head, service (to), shot upstairs (a), sixty-nine, slob your knob, smile like a donut, smoke, smoke your beef, soil your knees, spray your tonsils, suck, suck off, suck your sugar stick, swallow your sword, swallow cock, swap spit, talk in to the mic, tip, tongue, trick off (to), whistle, whomp it up, whoof it, worship at the altar, wring it dry, yodel, yummy it down, zipper sex

Femme

SEE ALSO EFFEMINATE MALE, BUTCH

Historically, femmes were lesbians who presented traditionally feminine gender traits and complimented their more masculine expressing partners, Butches. The definition has now expanded to acknowledge Femme as an independent gender choice.

Fairy Lady, femme, girly-girl, glam girl, high femme, lipstick lesbian, low femme, nice lady, stone femme, uber femme, ultra femme,

High femme vs low femme: professional manicure and skirts versus nail clippers and jeans.

Fetish(es) with Related Terms

Fetish: from the Portuguese feitico *for religious relic; a source of reverence and fascination. This in turn derived from* facticius, *Latin for artificial and* facere, *to do. Psychoanalysts later applied the term to body parts and clothing as sexual sources of obsession, orsomething, such as a material object or a nonsexual part of the body, that arouses sexual desire and may become necessary for sexual gratification. Modern psychiatry no longer refers to fetishistic activity as perversion but rather as paraphilia, from the Greek* para *(to the side of) and* philia *(love).*

abrasion, accident prone, addiction, adult basics, age play, algophilia, alternate proclivity, animal sex, animal training, a.s.b. (alt.sex. bondate), ass play, aural sex, Auto, auto-erotic asphyxiation, axillisma, baby play, bagpiping, ball play, ball torture, bars, bdsm,

Accident prone: A closeted SM player who blames repeated bruises and welts on falls or other accidents.
Axillisma: derives from axilla, *use of the armpit for sex.*
BDSM: "bondage/discipline/sadomasochism."
Bear: gay term for a heavy-set, hairy man (see Bear*).*

bears/bear culture, beating, begging, beginner, bent, bestiality, bigamy, birching, blade (knife games), blindfolds, blood sports, bodyshaving, body worship, bondage, bondage and discipline/ b&d, boots/boot-licking, branding, breath/breath control /breath games, breather, brown showers, bulletin boards, burial, butch, butt plug, caning, castration, cat, CBT, chainmail, chastity belts, chubby chaser,

Bondage: from the Latin bondagium, *to occupy or inhabit.*
Breather: obscene phone caller.
CBT: fetish culture frequently uses abbreviations or acronyms for specific practices, in this case "cock and ball torture."
Cigar daddy: a butch stogie-smoker.

cigarettes, cigar daddy, cigars, circumcision, clubs, cock torture, code words/codes, collegiate fucking, consenting adults, control scenes, coprophagy, coprophilia, corporal punishment/CP, corsets, cowboys, crops, cross-dressing, crucifixion, cub (a young bear), cunt torture, cupping, cutting, daddy, denim, dental dam, dependence, depilation, diapers, dildoes, discipline, dog training, dom (dominant), dominance/submission, dominatrix, double ender (a dildo with two insertive ends), douching, drag, dungeon, electricity, electrotorture, enemas, English, English arts, English culture, English vice, ephebophilia, equipment, execution scenes, exhibitionism, explicitness, extreme, fantasy, farms, feces, feet, femme, fist-fucking, fisting, fladge, flagellation, flake, flash(er), flat-fucking, flogging, flush, foot fetishism, foot-licking, footwear, force-feeding, fist-fucking, fisting,

Coprophagy: copro *(feces) and* phagy *(eating).*
Ephebophilia: fetishizization of teenagers.
The English vice: a American term for sado-masochism.
Freak fuck: objective of individuals who seek out physically deformed partners.
handballing: vaginal or anal penetration with the fist.

 foreskins/foreskin worship, frazzle, freak fuck, French, French maid, frottism, furniture, gags, gas masks, gender play, gender-bending, gender-fucking, genitorture, girls, gloves, golden shower(s), Greek, hafada, hair, handballing, handcuffs, hankies, hanky codes, harnesses, heavy scenes, hermaphrodites, hosiery, hospital, hue, humiliation, ingulfing, immobilization, in rôle, infantilism, injury,

Hafada: a piercing through the upper part of the scrotum.
ldu: leather, denim, uniform.
Infantilism: one who enjoys acting like a baby.
Lorum: a piercing through the skin on the underside of the penis.

intersex, inversion, jewellry, jocks, kicking, kink(y), knots, lace into, lashing, latex, lather, ldu, leather, leather queen, leather sex, leatherwork, leg work, lingerie, lorum, maids, mamock, masochism, master/ slave scenes, masturbation, mature scenes, meatflasher, menstrual play/scenes, mess, mild and bitter, military, mind fucking/games, mistress, motorcycles, Mr. Whippy, mummification, muscle, mute/mutism, nannies, nappies, naturism, necrophilia, needles, negotiation, new guard, nipple/tit clamps,

Mild and bitter: a catty reference to S&M.
Mr. Whippy/fladge: flagellation.
P.E: "power exchange," a master-slave relationship.

nipple torture, noses, novice, nudism, mul, nurses, nuts, old guard, oral sex, orgasm control, otter, outdoor scenes, paddles/ paddling, pain/pain games, pansexuality, panic, panties, pantyhose, P.E., pedophilia, Peeping Tom, percussion play, perversions, petticoat discipline, phone lines/sex, photographs, physical limits, piercing, piss, piss fest/play, play, playroom, pleasure and pain, ponies, poppers, porn, predilections, Prince Albert/P.A.,

PHOTO: DIANNE WHELAN

Prince Albert/P.A.: a piercing through the glans of the penis.
PT: physical training.
Quirt: a long coaching whip.

Princeton rub, privacy, professional dominance, PT, punching, punishment, quirt, R/S, rape scenes, raunch, reality, recreational drugs, regalia, restraints, rib roast, Roman culture, Rape fantasy, rough trade, rubber, rubber queen, S&M/ SM/sado-masochism, sadie-masie, sadism, safe, Safe Sane, and Consensual, safeword, sane, scarification, scat, scenes, scourging, self-bondage, sensations, sensory deprivation, shackles, shaving, she-males, shit, shoes, showers,

R/S: rough sex.
Rubber queen: a rubber fetishist.
Shrimping: toe sucking.
Strap-ons: dildos, usually referring to those used by women penetrating others
(women or men).
Sub/subby: submissive.
Tats: tatoos.
TPE: "total power exchange," describing a full-time (24/7) mistress/master-slave
relationship.

shrimping, skinheads, slavery, slings, smoddler & smoldster, smoking, socks, sodomy, spanking, splashing, stiletto heels, stockings, strangling, strap-ons, straps, student/teacher scenes, sub/subby, submission, suffocation,

Sado-masochism: from the Marquis de Sade
(1740-1814), a famous pain inflicter, and
Leopold von Sacher-Masoch (1876-1895),
who documented the pleasures of being
injured or ridiculed in his novels.
Modern SM culture emphasizes consent and
safety in all practices through verbal and
sometimes written contracts, as negotiated by
both partners. A safe word signal or stop word
indicates that the particular activity or "scene" must stop immediately when uttered
by either participant.

suspense, suspension, Swedish culture, swingers, switch, tats, tattooing, temperature play, tickling, tied down, tied up, tightbuck, tit torture/work, toes, toilet, top (bottom), toys, TPE, training, transgender, transsexual, transvestite, twisty, uniforms, urethral play, vaginal fisting, vanilla, video play, voyeurism, water sports, weenie-wagging, whips, whipping, wigs, withdrawal syndrome, wrestling, youth, zoophilia

WS (water sports) in personal ads does not describe swimming or water-skiing, but rather urophilia, a love of urine.

> *"Whoever allows himself to be whipped, deserves to be whipped."*
> —*Ritter Leopold von Sacher-Masoch*

Flatus (to Pass)

Included as a category here because it often occurs in bed.

backfire, backtalk, barking spiders, beef, blast, blow a fart, blow off, blow the horn, botch, break the sound barrier, break wind, break wind backwards, breeze, buck snort, burn bad powder, burn(t) cheese, buzz, carminate, crack a fart, crepitate, cut a fart, cut one, cut the cheese, drop a beast, drop a rose, drop a thumper, fart, fice, fizzle, flatulate, float an air-biscuit, fluff, foist, guff, gurk, honk, lay a fart, leave a whiff, let fly, let off, let one go, make a noise, make a rude noise, make wind, pass air, pass gas, pass wind, pffft, poot, puff, pump, pussywhistle, raise wind, release one, rump, scape, shoot rabbits, sneeze, talk German, through cough, toot, trump, vent

Break wind: the politest term for a subject best avoided or heard in polite company.
Pussywhistle: A pussy fart expelled after vaginal sex or certain yoga positions.

Fondle

SEE ALSO CARESS, KISS

These terms generally suggest rough, exploitative, or unwanted touch.

all over someone (be), bring on, bumble, canoodle, caterwaul, climb all over, clitorize, cock pluck, cop a feel, diddle, do homework, do some nether work, eat with the hands, explore the beads, feel up, fiddle, finger, finger fuck, firkytoodle, frisk, frothis, fudge, fumble, futz around, get your hand on it, get to first base, go on bush patrol, grab, grab ass, grabble, grope, handle, have foreplay, have hand trouble, have a petting party, honk, horn, huddle, jack, jam, love up, make out, manhandle, maul/mauling, meddle with, mess about, mouse, mug up, neck (with), nudge, nug, paddle, paw, peck and neck, pet, pet up, pinkie, pitch honey, play footsie, play grab ass,

Diddle: in the 19th century, this term meant to copulate but now means to masturbate yourself or another.
Maulmauling: a bear molestation.
Pet: a noun suggesting favourite, but is also used as a verb. More common in the 1950s and '60s ("heavy petting").

lay stink(y)-finger, practice heavy petting, practice in the milky way, practice sexual foreplay, read Braille, reef, rub, rummage, sample, sexaminate, slap and tickle, sprunch, spunk up, stroke, take your pulse, thumb, tip the middle finger, touch one up, touch up, toy with, trifle with, turn on

Foreskin

(SEE ALSO PENIS, CIRCUMCIZED)

banana skin, blinds, Bobby's anorak, Canadian bacon, cavalier, cock collar, coliseum curtains, convertible vs. hardtop, curtains, end, extra skin, fiveskin, helmet pelmet, lace, lace curtains, midnight lace, onion skin, opera cape, prepuce, Principal Skinner, sheath, snapper, turtleneck sweater, whickerbill, zoot

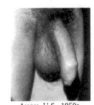

ANON. U.S., 1950s.
THOMAS WAUGH COLLECTION

Draw the blinds: pull back the foreskin.
Principal Skinner: penis with foreskin. Refers to a character, the much mocked
school principal, on TV's The Simpsons.

Four-Letter Words
A 20th-century euphemism for "swear words" of a sexual or scatalogical nature, the
most potent and forbidden being fuck.
arse, cock, cunt, dick, fart, fuck, homo, piss, quim, shit, tits, turd,
twat

> *Top 10 taboo terms of all-time: 1. motherfucker; 2. cocksucker; 3. fuck; 4. pussy;*
> *5. cunt; 6. prick; 7. cock; 8; bastard; 9. son of a bitch; 10. asshole*
—*Source: T.B. Jay, Kent State University, published in* Maledicta Journal of Erotic
Language

The Seven Forbidden Words: Before Howard Stern pushed the envelope, there were
only seven obscene words the FCC (Federal Communicaitons Commission) deemed
unmentionable on Amercian radio: shit, piss, fuck, cunt, cocksucker, motherfucker *and* tits.

Frigid
Once used medically, now a rarely used term for a sexually unresponsive woman.
Gay men and women now use many of these terms to describe boring sexual part-
ners.
anorgasmic, bed death (suffers from), bed swerver, chilly, cold,
cold fish, colder than a witch's tit, dead, dead down there, dysfunctional, freezy, hates sex, ice queen, icebox, icy, inhibited,
inorgasmic, just lies there, like a fish, like an ice cube, passion-
less, ribena on toast, Sno-cone, princess (a), stone, undersexed,
unresponsive, uptight

Bed death: refers to a lesbian relationship which has become sexless.

Gaydar
The intuitive sensing of other gays, or the sense that someone you've met is gay.
Dykedar, OGT, Ping

Dykedar: the lesbian version of gaydar.
OGT: "obviously gay trait."
Ping: transgender version of gaydar.

Gay Male (Hidden): See Closet Case

Gay Male
SEE ALSO COME OUT OF THE CLOSET, CLOSET CASE, FELLATIO (ONE WHO PERFORMS), GAY (TO HIDE YOUR HOMOSEXUALITY), SODOMY, SODOMITE, SODOMIZE

Most of these terms are derogatory, though gay liberation has seen the reappropriation of terms like queer *and* fag *by gay men who now use them defiantly.*

4-2-9, 71s'er, A-gay, aberration, active, active sodomist, aesthete, afgay, ag-fay, aggie,

4-2-9: spells gay on the telephone dial.
71s'er: refers to an 1871 German penal code banning homosexuality.
A-gay: an "A-list" gay man who has money, looks, and power.
Aggie: a gay sailor.

alternaqueer, Amyl queen, anal buccaneer, anal jabber, androtrope, angel, ansy-pay, antiman, ass bandit, ass fucker, ass king, ass leech, ass licker, ass man, ass peddler, ass pirate, ass pro, ass watcher, aunt eater, auntie, auntie Queen, buddy/fuck buddy,

Amyl queen: a gay man who likes poppers (amyl nitrate).
Angel food: a gay male or sexual partner who is in the Air Force.
Antiman: a Caribbean gay male.
Asshole buddy/fuck buddy: a non-romantic sexual friendship.
Auntie queen: a young man who likes older men.

BB, baby, bachelor, back scuttler, backdoor bandit, backdoor buddy, backgammon player, backside artist, badling, bag, banana, bandit, bang artist, banjy boy, bat boy, batty battyman, beachcomber, bean queen, bear, beefer, belle, belle boy, belly

queen, bender, benderast, bent as a boomerang, bent as a nine
bob note, bent shot, bent wrist, berdache, Bertie, Betty, bimbo,
birdie, bitch, blade, block boy, blue, blue discharger,

BB: bum boy.
Banjy boy/block boy: a gay male hip hop guy who dresses straight.
Bean queen: a Mexican gay man.
Belly queen: likes six-packs.
*Blue discharger: refers to the colour of paper on which WWII discharges for gay
men were written.*
Bog queen: frequents toilets.
Bondage queen: likes to be tied up.

bog queen, bois, bonco, bondage queen, bone queen, bone
smuggler, bone stroker, booty-buffer, bottom, bottomite, botty
boy/man/officer, boy, boy scout, boy scout queen, boy toy, boy-
ass, Boys 'R Us, boyz, Brighton Pier, broken wristed, bronco,
broncobuster, bronzer, brown hatter, brown trout, brown queen
(bottom), brownie, Bruce, brucey, Bruthey, bufty, bufu, bufus,
bugger,

Boys 'R Us: a popular U.S. t-shirt.
*Bugger: used since the 16th century; an example of ethnic slurring in sexual slang,
as the "evil" Bulgars were said to practice the vice of sodomy.*

bum-bandit, bum-chum, bumboy, bumpy, bun duster, bunny
boy, bunter, butch, butt pirate, buttboy, buttercup, butterfly, buttfuck buddy, buttfucker, buzzer, bwoy, cakpipe cosmonaut, cake
boy, cake eater, camp, camp bitch, camp as a row of tents,
Canadian, cannibal, capon, cart tart/trolley dolly, Castro clone,
cat, catamite, catch(er), Charlie, chichi, chicken, chicken hawk,
chicken queen, chimney sweep, chirujo, chocolate bandit, cho-
rus boy,

cart tart/trolley dolly: a gay airline steward.
*chicken queen: one who likes underage boys (or an older gay man with a penchant
for younger).*

Chutney ferret: a modern British term, suggesting one who ferrets out fecal matter (resembling chutney), a reference to anal sex.

chuffer, chum-chum, church member, Chutney ferret, cissy/sissy, clay court specialist, clear, clone, closet case, closet homosexual, closet queen, closet queer, cloven hoofter, cock queen, cock sucka, cockeater,

OSCAR WILDE

Clear: exclusively gay.
Clone: a medical term suggesting genetic sameness, described a uniform look for gay men in the 1970s: short hair, moustache, bomber jacket, muscular body, tight jeans.
Closet: in the 20th century, commonly refers to homosexuality which is hidden, but may refer to other cloaked or disavowed identities: i.e., closet Commie, or closet liberal.
Dock sucka/Miss Thang/sweet/punk: African-American slang for a gay male.

cockpipe, cocksucker, collar, collar and cuff, colon commando, come/cum freak, companion, con, confirmed bachelor, cookie pusher, coolie, cornflakes, cornholer, cosmonaut, cot betty, cot queen, counter jumper, cowboy, crafty butcher, cream puff, cornhole cowboy, crevice courier, cruiser, cuca, cupcake, curry queen, cut sleeves,

Curry queer: one who likes South Asian men.
Cut sleeves: In Chinese, the phrase, tuan hsiu *applies to male homosexuality. From the story of Emperor Ai-ti (6 B.C.-A.D. 2) whose favoured young boy fell asleep on the sleeve of his robe. The emperor cut off the sleeves of his robe rather than disturb the sleeping boy.*
Deedee: a Hindi term.
Dangle queen: shows off crotch in tight pants.
Dolly domestic: shacked-up gay male.
Drama queen: a histrionic gay man.

daffodil, daisy, dandy, dangle queen, date hunter, daughter, dead-

eye dick, debutante, deviate, dick(ie)-licker, dinge, din-
ter, dirt tamper, disciple of Oscar Wilde, dodgy dea-
con, dolly domestic, dool, double-barrelled ghee, double ribs, drama queen, drugstore cowboy, duchess,
duckey, dung-puncher, Dutch boy, Dyke Tyke, Dyna, E

queen, eclair queen, eer-quay, effeminate male/effie, enema bandit, epicene, Esther, Ethel, eyeball queen, fag, fagateeny, faggart,
faggo, faggot, faggotress, fagola, fairy, fairy lady, family member,
fancypants, farg, fart catcher, father fucker, faygeleh, feather spitter, felch queen, felcher, fembo, femme, fenne, fey, Finocchio,
flag, flaggott, flamer, flaming queen, flaming queer, flamingo,

E queen/X queen: ecstasy user.
Eclair queen: a rich gay man.
Esther: a Jewish gay man.
Eyeball queen: a gawker of good-looking men.
Faggo: popularized by comedian Scott Thompson (Kids in the Hall), *who suggest-*
ed the Christian right's objection to faggots is the use of the letter "t" and its ressem-
blance to the cross.

Many early terms link homosexuality with effeminacy, or the practice of anal sex or
fellatio.

Faygeleh: Yiddish for gay male.
Freak: an African-American term for a male homosexual.
Friend of Dorothy: reference to Dorothy from The Wizard of Oz, *much beloved by*
gays("I have a feeling we're not in Kansas anymore").
Frog queen: likes French or Quebecois men.

Faggot as a term for gay males may derive from the Old French faget *or a bundle*
of twigs used for burning (deviants including homosexuals were once burnt at the
stake). An alternate source may be fagge, *a Middle English term for broken thread.*
It later meant leftover remnant or reject, in a pejorative sense. Faggot also came to
mean woman in the 1500s.

flicker, flit, flor, flower, flute, fluter, flyball, flyfisher, fooper, four
letter man, freak, freckle-puncher, freep, fresh fruit, fribble,

friend of Dorothy, frit, frog queen , fruit, fruit fly, fruit picker, fruit plate, fruitcake, fruits, fruitter, fu, fuff, fudge packer, fut-tbucker, GAM, gander, Ganymede, gashead, gay, gay as a goose, gay as pink ink, gay boy, gay guy, gay man, gaybert, gayblade, gaydeer, caught on the, gaysexual, GBM, gear, gear box, gentle-man of the backdoor, gentlemiss, ginga, ginger beer, girl, girl-friend, girlie, glamazon, gobbler,

GBM: gay black male; GOM/GAM: gay Oriental/Asian male; GWM: gay white male.
Ginger beer: rhymes with queer.

golden queen/golden shower queen (likes urine), gom, gonsel, good buddy, government inspected meat (military man), gravy pumper, Greek, green and yellow fellow, green suit, green queen (frequents parks), gunsel/gonsil/gonzel/goncel/guntzel/gunzl, guppie, Gussie, gutfucker, GWM,

gunsel/gonsil/gonzel/goncel/guntzel/gunzl: 1900s Yiddish for gosling, suggesting a young passive gay male.
Gay: Once used in the 16th century to describe a promiscuous female, by the 1920s homosexual men started to use this word to describe themselves. From the 1970s on, in the U.S., U.K., Australia, and Canada, it is the standard reference both as an adjective and a noun.

hair pin, hairy Mary, hairburner, hairy fairy, happy-lad-lover, haricot, harry hoof, hat, he-she, hen hussy, Hershey bar (boy), hesh, him-her, himmer,

Hairburner: a gay male hairdresser.
Hitchhiker on the Hershey highway: refers to both chocolate and the anus. This modern expression links the gay man (hitchhiker) and anal intercourse.
HIT: "Homo in training."
HP (homee palare): Polari for gay male.

HIT, hitchhiker on the Hershey highway, hock, hodgie, home-boy, homie, homintern, homo, homogenic, homophile, homo-

sexual, homosexualist, horse's hoof, HP, huckle, indorser, insertee, insertor, inspector of manholes, intestinal tourist, invert,
Irish by birth but Greek by injection, iron (hoof), jag, jaisy, jaw
queer/queen, Jeanie-boy, Jenny, Jenny Willocks, jere, Joan of
Arc, jobby jabber, jocker, jockey, joey, jolly, joy boy, kazoonie,
killer queen, King Lear, kisser, kweer, KY cowboy, KY queen,
label queen, lacy, lad-lass, lamb, larro, lavender boy,

"The word 'homosexual' itself is a bastard term compounded of Greek and Latin elements." —H. Havelock Ellis

Jenny Willocks: A Scottish term for a bottom.
Label queen: favours designer clothes.
Killer queen: military man
KY cowboy: refers to the lubricant KY, used by men for anal intercourse.

lean cuisine queen, leather daddy, leather queen, left-footer, left-
handed, lick-box, lilac, lily, limp wrist, lisper, lithper, little dear,
Lizzie boy, lost at sea, lumberjack, lunch puncher, M4M, macho
man, mahn, main queen, malkin, mamapoule, mandrake, man's
man, mardie, margarita, marge, Margery, marico, mariposa,
Mary/Mary Ann/Blanche/Rose etc., mattress-muncher,

Lean cuisine queen: perpetually on a diet.
Lost at sea: "situationally" gay, as when in prison.
M4M: "Man for men."
Margarita/maricon/mariposa: Spanish slang for gay male meaning daisy, faggot, and butterfly, respectively.
Mary/Mary Ann/Blanche/Rose, etc.: a woman's name used to indicate a gay man.
Maxwell: a gay hipster.
Mean queen: gay man into S&M.
Midnight queen: one who likes African-Americans.
Miss Thing: a camp expression for a gay male.

Maud, Mavis, Maxwell, meacocke, mean queen, meat hound,
member of the brown family, member of the union, midger,
midnight cowboy, midnight queen, milksop, mince, mincer,

miner, Minnie, mintie, misfit, miss, Miss Nancy, Miss Thang, Miss Thing, Miss USO, mitten queen, mo/moe, moff(y), Molly, molly mop, mollycoddle, mophrodite, mother, MOTSS, mouser, mud-packer, muppet, muscle queen, musical, muzzle, namby pamby, Nan boy, Nance, Nancy, nancy boy, Nancy Dawson, Nancy Homey, Navy Cake,

Miss USO: gay in the military.
Mitten queen: masturbation fan.
MOTSS: "member of the same sex."
Muscle queen: fan of bodybuilders or well-built types.
Nance (American) and Nancy (U.K.): terms used to refer to an effeminate male
homosexual through use of a woman's name; first used in the 1800s.

Nellie fag, Nelly, neon-carrier, nephew, Neptune's daughter, neuter gender, nice Nellie, nick nack, nigh enough, night sneakers, no bullfighter, nola, nudger, odd, oddball, omi-paloni, one of the boys, one of those, one of us, one-way street, one who bats for the other team, one who camps about, one who camps it up, one who dresses on the left, one who has a weakness for boys, one who is abnormal, one who is funny, one who is in the life, one who is left-handed, one who is light footed, one who is light on his toes,

ANON. GERMANY, C. 1920s.
THOMAS WAUGH COLLECTION

60

Neptune's daughter: a gay sailor.
Oscar and to oscarize (to make homosexual): refer to the 19th-century British
writer Oscar Wilde, who was tried and imprisoned for committing "gross indecen-
cy" with a younger male.

one who is like that, one with alternative proclivity/sexuality, one who is on the other bus, one who is out, one who is out of the closet, one who is passive, one who is peculiar, one who is queer as a three-dollar bill, one who is queer as a three-pound note, one who is queer as an electric walking stick, one who takes little interest in the opposite sex, one who is that way, one who is that way inclined, one who is unmarried, one who wears Dick's hat-band, oofterpa, orchid eater, Oscar, packer, pansified, pansy, panty,

oofterpa: pig latin for poofter.
Pansy: a delicate, pretty flower, used to refer to an effeminate gay man since the
early 1900s.
Paris brothers: gay brothers/twins.
Payoff queen: one who pays for sex.
Pillow-biter: refers to the passive male partner in anal sex who bites the pillow to
stifle cries of pain or pleasure while being penetrated.

waist, pap mouth, Paris brothers, pash, pato, payoff queen, peanut buffer, peanut packer, pee Willie, Percy, Perry Como, perv, pervert, petal, petal pix(ie), Peter Pansy, peter puffer, petit ami, pickle kisser, pillow-biter, pilot of the chocolate runway, pineapple, pink pound, pipefitter, piss-hole bandit, pitch(er), pix, pixy, poggler, pogue, poison queen, pole pleaser, ponce, poo per-colator, pood, poof, pooftah, poofter, poonce, poove, pouffe, pow-der puff, precious, pretty boy, princess, priss queen, privy queen, prune-pusher, puff, punk, putty pusher,

Perry Como: rhymes with homo.
Poison queen: engages in vicious gossip.
Poof: this term, and its variations poofter and pooftah are commonly used in

Britain and Australia and come from pouffe, *French for puff.*
Priss queen: a snooty gay man.
Privy queen: likes toilet sex.

punce, punk, pure silk, puss gentleman, pussy, pussy Nellie, Q., QUIT,

Pure silk: a 1960s African-American term for a gay man.
QUIT: "queer under intensive training."
Quaggot: queer faggot.
Queen for a day: a man who has occasional gay sex.
Queen of Scotch: a gay alcoholic.

quaggot, quean, queanie, queen, queen for a day, Queen of Scotch, queer, queer as a coot(e), queerie, queervert, quince, rabbit, radical fairy, raging Queer, rainbow beard, receiver, rectal researcher, rectal Romeo, red neck tie, renter, ribbon clerk, rice queen, rim warrior, rimadona, ring jocket, ring rebel, roaring poofter, roger ramjet, rump ranger, sausage jockey, sausage smuggler, scat queen, scene queen/club queen/queen of clubs, roger ramjet, screamer/screecher, screaming fairy, seafood, semen demon, Seymour, sgo, shandy, she, she-he, she-man, shim, shirt-lifter, shit-stabber, shit-puncher, shore dinner, sicko, sings in the choir, sis, sissy, sissy britches, sister, size queen, skippy, snake handler, snap, snap diva, snapper, snow queen,

Scat queen: likes feces.
Scene queen/club queen/queen of clubs: likes partying.
Scout queen: pretends to be asleep during gay sex.
Seafood: an example of a food metaphor, in this case, gay male slang for a marine or sailor. Shore dinner *and* tuna *are other examples.*
Snow queen: takes cocaine.
Snowflake queen: likes to be ejaculated on.
Soda fountain queen: likes golden showers.

snowflake queen, so, soapy, sod, soda fountain queen, sodomite, softie, spade queen (likes black men), spag fag (likes Italians), sperm burper, sphincter boy, spintry, spurge, steam queen (likes the baths), steamer, stern-wheeler, sweater queer, swedish, sweet, sweetcorn shiner, sweetie, swish, tailgunner, tapette, that way, thing, third, third sexer, thithy, three-dollar bill, three-legged beaver, three-letter man,

Spag fag: likes Italians.
Steam queen: likes the baths.
Sweater queer: a preppy gay male.
Thithy: a lisping variant of sissy, as it was once assumed that all gay men lisped.
Three-letter man: U.S. term from the 1930s; refers to earning activity letters on your college sweater—in this case, f-a-g.

Tinkerbelle, tinkle tinkle, Tinky Winky, toe jam queen, token fag/queen, Tommy Dodd, tonk, tooti-frootie, top, torah queen, trick, trouser bandit, truck driver, tubesteak tarzan, turd-bandit, turd-burglar, turd-dinter, turd-packer, turd-puncher, Turk, twank, twiddlepoop, twink, twinkle toes, twit, twixter, two-spirited, uffi-may, Uncle, undercover agent/man, uphill gardener, Uranian, Uranist, urning, Vaseline boy,

Tinky Winky: name of the character from the children's TV program Teletubbies *rumoured to be gay (because he is lavender in colour and carries a "magic bag").*
Uranian: from the Greek ouranios *(heavenly); was used in the late 1800s, probably because Uranus contains the word* anus.
Water chestnut: gay Japanese.
Water Lily: gay Englishman.
Zebrajox: black guys who like white guys (and vice versa).
Feminizing labels are often used when referring to another gay man. For example: she, girl, girlfriend, bitch, slut, slutleena, Miss Thing, Mary, whorella. *These terms often express a queer mix of both spite and community.*

Vegemite valley visitor, vegetarian, waiter, water chestnut, water Lily, weak sister, weird(ie), whoops boy, whoopsie, wide receiver, windjammer, wife, Willie, Willie Boy, windjammer, woman, wonk, woof, woofter, woolly woofter, wrong, X-queen, yoo-hoo boy, zebrajox

Gay Male (Post-Youth/Older)

These terms are mostly derogatory and reflect the unfortunate ageism in some parts of the gay community.

afghan, aging actress, antique, aunt, Aunt Matilda, auntie, Auntie Mame, chicken hawk, chin strap, coffin dodger, corpse, crow, Dad, Daddy, dirty mind, dowager, elderberry, fallen star, flapper, fleabagger, fossil, fungus, geritol set, grand duchess, grandma, grave sniffer, gray lady, grey wolf, Grimm's fairy,

Daddy: an older gay male, often the object of desire of a much younger guy.
Ladder: a old gent into young lads.
Wrinkle queen: someone who likes sex with older men.

jouster, ladder, leather bag/purse, mama gaga, nudger, old girl, old goat, old hen, old queen, old queer, old thing, over-ripe fruit, pensioner, prime-timer, prune, rancid flavour, rancid flower, sea hag, toad, toff omee, troll, wheelchair set, witch, wrinkle queen, zook

Gay (to Hide your Homosexuality)

butch it up, in the glass closet (to be), in the iron closet, lose your gender, on the down low, perform a nellyectomy, stay in the closet, take the veil, try to pass, wear a cut-glass veil, wear a mourning veil

On the down low: African-American term for acting straight in public.
Take the veil: to get married.

Gay Sex Venues
(and terms related to activities there)

SEE ALSO BROTHEL, PORNOGRAPHY

abdicate, alfresco, altar room, aquarium, back slums, backroom, bagnio, ballroom, bathhouse, baths (the), bathsheba, birthday party (orgy), boys' club, buddy booths, bush (push push in the), bushes (the), cafeteria, camp, church, circuit (the), common bawdy house,

Abdicate: to leave a toilet when a cop is on duty.
Alfresco: Italian for outside, in the fresh air.
Aquarium: a corner where lesbians congregate in a gay bar.
Bathsheba: one who frequents the baths.
Camp: place where gay and lesbian teens hang out.

cottage, crib, Crisco disco, cruising spot, cruisy, dark room, den of sin, dog's match, dunes (do the), extra-friendly skies, fairy glen, fairy-go-round, flush factory, French Embassy, fruit loop,

Boys' club, church, crib, den of sin, flush factory, and the tub(s) are all synonyms for a bathhouse.
Cottage: a modern English expression for a public bathroom or urinal. Cottaging refers to having sex in a lavatory.
fruit loop: a car cruising area.

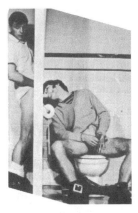

fruit stand, gay ghetto, glory-hole, great outdoors (enjoy the), grope room, Hershey Bar, hygiene hall, j/o/jack off/jerk off club, lollipop stop, make a milk run (to), meat-packing district, meat rack, mecca, mile-high club, musical chairs,

Extra-friendly skies/mile-high club: sex on airplanes.
Glory hole: a hole cut into a bathroom or other wall to allow access to a penis or other body part.
Lollipop stop: highway rest stop.
Musical chairs: refers to cruising in a movie theatre.
Make a milk run: visit a toilet.
Out gardening: having sex in a park.

nature (enjoy), orgy room, our lady of the vapours, out gardening (having sex in a park), outdoor recreation, park (the), penile colony, pickle park, pier (visit the), pig room, playroom/play space, porn theatre, pussy palace, Ruth Ann's, sauna, sex shop, skin room, slurp ramp, strip joint, teahouse, tearoom, toilet, throne room, tub(s), vaseline villa, video booths, waterfront (work the), wharf (visit the), zipper club

Genitalia, Female (General)

SEE ALSO CLITORIS, LABIA, VAGINA

Much of the slang for female genitalia was originally invented by straight men and suggests a disinterest in distinguishing among specific parts of the female anatomy: pudendum, labia, vagina, uterus. *Many terms are used interchangeably and have been appropriated by gay men to describe the anus.*

ace, ace of spades, agility, antipodies, basket, bazaar, bazoo, bearded clam, beauty spot, beaver, beef, belly, between the legs, bit, black badger, blackness, bont, boody, booty, bore, box, bread, bucket, budget, bug, bun(ny), burning shame, C,

Beaver: North American term from the 1960s, often used in pornographic materials: i.e., beaver shots, where pubic hair and the vagina are displayed.
C: an example of one letter used as a substitute for a "dirty word," in this case cunt.

cabbage, cabbage field, cabbage patch, cachancha, cake, can, Cape Horn, carnal parts, carnal trap, cauliflower, cellar, centre of bliss, centre of joy, cherry, chink, chuff, chunk, churn, civet, cockles, cockpit, codger, conny, constable, contrapunctum, conundrum, cony/conny, cooch, cookie, coot, cooze, corner, coyote, crack, cradle, crotch, cunning, cunnus, cunny, cunt, Cupid's alley, Cupid's cave, Cupid's corner, cushion, date, diddly pout, dimple, ditch, dot, doughnut, et cetera, Eve's custom house, eye, fan, fancy bit, fanny, feet, femininity, fern, fig, Fitz, flange, flesh, front bottom, front door, front parlour, front passage, front porch,

Coot: 20th-century American term; related to cooze.
Fanny: in the U.S., currently means buttocks, but was first used in the U.K. as a
euphemism for female genitals. It may have its origin in the novel Fanny Hill:
Memoirs of a Woman of Pleasure, *written by John Cleland in 1749.*
Furburger: born in 1960s American burger-boom; a term for vulva used by ham-
burger-loving college students. Hairburger *is a variant.*

front window, front-bum, fudd, furburger, futy, gadooch, gap, gape,
garden, gash, gentleman's delight,
gentleman's garden, golden doughnut, goods (the), growler, gusset,
gutted rabbit, gym, ha'penny, hair
pie, hairburger, hairy losso, hairy
magnet, hide, hogeye, hole, honeypot, hooch, hoop, hotel, ivory gate,
jam, jelly-roll, Joe Hunt, kettle, key-
hole, kitchen, kitty, lap, leather, little sister, little Ms. Peach, loins,
long eye, Lord knows what, low-
lands, madge, magnet,

Merkin: 17th-century term for a pubic wig, later a slang term for the female geni-
tals, possibly derived from malkin, *which was used to describe an untidy, lower-*
class woman.

manometer, marble arch, masterpiece, meat, merchandise,
merkin, mich, Michael, mickey, minge, mole catcher, money,
moneymaker, monkey, mons pubis, mons veneris, mortar, mott,
mound, mound of Venus, muff, mushroom, mutt, mutton,
nasty, naughty bits, nether regions, nick, noose, notch, O, old
thing, orifice, ornament, pan, paradise, parts, pas touche, patch,
piece, pink bits, piss slit, pisser, pit, playing field, pot, pranny,
private parts, pudenda, pulpit, pussy, quaint, quarry, quid, quiff,
quim, quiro, rose, rubyfruit, saddle,

Pas touche: 20th-century Québec Cree, meaning "don't touch."
Rubyfruit: popularized in Rubyfruit Jungle, *a classic lesbian novel by American author Rita Mae Brown.*
Twat (twot): first used in the 17th century to signify the female genitals, but origins unknown.

scratch, seminary, slash, slit, slot, sluice, snatch, spot, squirrel, sweet potato pie, thing, till, touch hole, trinket, twam (my), twat, twot, vag, valve, velvet glove, velvet vice, vertical smile, vulva, water engine, water worker, wee wee, whatsit, wheel, whim, whisker biscuit, whore winker, wound, wrinkle, yawn, you know, yum(s), zatch

Vulva: a current medical term for the female external genitalia. Latin for uterus.

Genitalia, Male (General)
SEE ALSO CROTCH, FORESKIN, GLANS, PENIS, SCROTUM, TESTICLES
Men have tended to be more lighthearted or vain in naming their own bits than when naming those of women.
abdomen, Adam's arsenal, affair, affairs, apparatus, appendage, auxiliary, bag of tricks, balls and bat, basket, basketful of meat, bat and balls, Big Jim and the twins, bread basket, boss and his

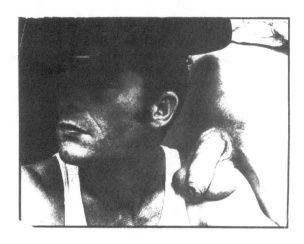

two helpers, box, boys, bulge, business,

"My boys need to breathe."
—*Kramer on TV's* Seinfeld, *on why he wears boxer shorts.*

Christ and two apostles, codpiece, concern, credentials, crotch, crotch rocket, crown jewels, dingbats, dohickies, dojiggers, down below, downstairs, droolies, engine, equipment, essentials, family jewels, fancy work, gear, groin, hairy wheel, ham and two eggs, holiday money, intimate parts, jewelry, kit, lady-ware, laundry, loins, lot, lower abdomen, luggage, manliness, match, mate, material part, meat and two vegetables, most precious part(s), Mr. Mulch, natura, naturalia, necessaries, nether parts, Netherlands, num-nums, okra and prunes, outfit, packet, parts, pencil and tassel, poperine pear, prack, prides, private parts, private property, privates, privities, rule-of-three, sausage and eggs, secret parts, shape, snack, stick and bangers, string and nuggets, tackle, thing, three-piece suit, tools, two dots and a dash, vessels, virilia, virility, vitals, ware, watch and seals, wedding kit, whatzis, wooter, works, zipperfish

Crown jewels (U.K.) and family jewels (U.S.): refer specifically to the testicles.
Three-piece suit: refers to the classic business uniform as well as to cock and balls.

Girlfriend

SEE ALSO SWEETHEART
Many of the terms used by lesbians borrow playfully from "wife." Girlfriend is also what a gay man, in a femmie / queenie moment, will call a male pal.
awful-wedded wife, ball and chain, best piece, better half, bitch, bit on the side, bitter half, block and tackle, blushing bride, body and soul, bride, CSP, carving knife,

"As your lover describes you, so you are"
—*Jeanette Winterson,* Sexing the Cherry

cheese and kisses, chick, chief of staff, close friend, close rela-

PHOTO: DIANNE WHELAN

tionship, common-law spouse, common-law spouse, common-law wife, companion, consort, constant companion, date, domestic partner, dona, Dutch, dutchess, firebell, flame, fork and knife, friend, front office, gal, GF, girl, headquarters, helpmate, Her Highness, her indoors, home cooking, homework, honey, inamorata, item, joy of my life, just good friends, lady, lady friend, lady wife, legal mate, life-mate, life-partner, little woman, lover, ma, ma chum, ma blonde, mare, mate, missis, missus (the), mother of pearl, Mrs., Ms. Right, my Queen, new friend, O and O, old bubble, old Dutch, old flame, old lady/OL, old saw, old woman/OW, other half, partner, plates and dishes, poker breaker, private property, rib, romance, roommate, secretary, sergeant major, significant other/sigot/sother, slave-driver, spouse, steady, struggle and strife, sweet momma, sweetheart, trouble and strife, true love, valentine, War Department, warden, wedded wench, wifey, wiff, woman, woman-friend, worry and strife

Ma blonde: French-Canadian slang for girlfriend. While not a word of queer origin, use of the feminine pronoun preceeding this heterosexual expression outs the speaker to everyone in earshot. Those who hear it, know she doesn't mean a girl who happens to be a friend. Also: Ma Chum.
O and O: "One and only."

Glans

SEE ALSO **PENIS**

Terms for glans are comparative and "rooted" in an urge to generalize and broaden the turn-on of the cock.

bald-headed hermit, bald-headed mouse, beautiful head, bellend, big purple head, blunt head, bobby's helmet, bombhead, bright red head, bright red knob, bulbous head, bulbous cockhead, bulging cockhead, bulp, cock-knuckle, command module, cone, corona, crown, curving head, deep purple cockhead, deep purple head, engorged knob, German helmet, head, heart, helmet, jewel, knob, knobby head, knot, large head, mushroom cap, mushroom head, mushroom-rigged, mushroom tip, onion, pink gland, pink knob, plum-coloured head, point, pointed head, radish, round glans, sensitive head, shiny head, slick head, swollen head, swollen knob, tender head, turnip, wide head

Bald-headed hermit: because it is hairless, solitary, and hides away from the foreskin.
Mushroom-rigged: a man with a large glans and small shaft.

Handsome/Attractive (Male)
SEE ALSO MUSCULAR, WELL-ENDOWED
The marketing of men as sexual objects is a growing phenomenon. This list continues to expand as consumers are inundated with erotic images of males.
A & F, Adonis, all that, babe, babe on wheels, baby's got it goin' on, babycakes, Baldwin, baller, Barney, bean hunk, beauty boy, Beef-a-roni, beefbot, beulah, biff, big boy, bit of all right, big-time operator, blazing, BND, body, boi, bona palone, bracelet, bruiser, brummy, buff boy, buffage, cake, candy ass, catalogue man, CD, centerfold, charmer, Chelsea boy, cock on the walk, cocksman, cock strong, crushman, cute daddy/hot daddy, cute number, cutie, daddio, Darth, demigod, dish, dreamboat, dude, dude on toast, dude on wheels, eye candy, face, fine, fine specimen, flawless, fly-boy, foine, freak daddy, funky ass, game gear, genxy, God, God's gift, golden boy, gorgism, GQ, he-man, HMA, hoochie, honey, hoss, hot number, hot shit,

A&F: someone who belongs in Abercrombie & Fitch's catalogue, known for its, attractive models.
Bona palone: Polari for hunk.
BLED: "Biteable, lickable, edible, doable."
BND: "Boy next door."
Bracelet: a cute young man on the arm of a drag queen.

CD: *"Cute daddy."*
CFB: *"Cute from behind."*
Darth: *Gay surfer slang for cute guy.*
HMA: *"Handsome man alert."*
GQ: *refers to someone good-looking enough to appear in the hackneed men's fashion magazine, GQ.*
MOMD: *"Man of my dreams."*
Monet: *like some paintings, most attractive from afar.*
P.C.: *"Prince Charming."*

ANON. FRANCE/TUNISIA, C. 1950.
THOMAS WAUGH COLLECTION

hot ticket, hottie/hotty, Howard, hubba-hubba, hunk, hunkasauraus, hunkorama, hunkster, Jackson, jock, joss/josster, living doll, loverboy, lunchy, mazeh, meat, model, MOMD, Monet, muffin, muscle muffin, nail, newbie, number, P.C., phat, pickup, piece, piece of ass, psq, rack, rat, ride, schwa, scenery, smasher, smooth daddy, snack, spunk, spunk rat, stallion, stud, studmuffin, talent, ten (a), trapper, trophy, tuna, twink/twinkie, unit, vanity smurf, X'er, young buck, young spunk, yummy pants

PSQ: *"Porn star quality."*
Unit: *a group of cute boys at a bar.*
Vanity smurf: *a man who checks himself out repeatedly in the gym mirror.*

Handsome Man (Adjectives)

and some, awesome, babelicious, beulah, blazing, bona, boomin, boyfriendly, bubble yum, choice, cornfed, cracker, DDFMG, delish, doable, drooly, drop dead (gorgeous), fagalicious, fagulous, fancy, fatal, fine(foyne), flavaful, flawless, flitchy, flossin', foxy, fuckable, ginchy, haveable, hot, hotcha, hub, hubba, humpin, humpy, hunky, in there, industrial, jinglin', mobile, oomphy, PT, right on time, saucalicious, scrumpable, sexational, sexy, sizzlin',

smokin', studly, suave, tasty, TDH, to-die-for, VAF, woof, would-
n't kick him out of bed

DDFMG: "Drop dead fuck-me gorgeous."
PT: "Prick teaser."
TDH: "Tall, dark, and handsome."
VAF: "Very attracive fag."

Heterosexual (Male or Female)

babymaker, Barbara (male), basher/gay-basher/queer-basher,
beard, butch sister, breeder, breeder fish, dash, dyke daddy, ex-
gay, fish wife, fag hag, fag magnet, fag stag, fish & chips,

Basher/gay-basher/queer-basher: violent homophobe.
Breeder: a contemporary derogatory term related to having children; likely repre-
sents a backlash to the many derogatory terms for gay.
Butch sister: gay slang for a straight man.
Dash: open to gay sex, but not gay identified.
Dyke daddy/ fag stag/lesbo lad: a straight man who likes gay men/lesbians.
Fag hag/fruit bat/fruit fly/gay goodess/queen bee/tse-tse: a straight woman who
likes gay men and has many gay male friends.

frock, fruit bat, fruit fly, GB, GG, gay goddess, het, hetero, het-
tie/hetty, HIT, homosensual, jam, Kinsey One, metrosexual,
mundane, NAFF, norm, normal, Norman Normal, not in the
Tate, princess with a pink wand, queen bee, queer straight, right-
handed, sappho daddy-o, sings in the choir, str8, straight,
straight but not narrow, straight-jacket (in a), stray (a), tourist,
townie, trade, tse-tse, vanilla, wanna be, zero

Fish wife: straight woman married to a gay man.
Fish & chips: wife and kids of a gay man.
Flavorless: hipster talk for straight.
GB/GG: genetic boy/girl.
HIT: homo in training.
Homosensual: a straight person who thinks gay.
Metrosexual: a straight urban guy with gay style.

NAFF: Polari for "Not available for fucking."
Queer straight/straight queer: a heterosexual person supportive of gay politics.
Sappho daddy-o: straight man who hangs out with lesbians.

HIV/AIDS: SEE STDs

Homosexuality

SEE ALSO GAY MALE, LESBIAN

Homosexuality, from the Greek homo, meaning the same, was first coined in the 19th century. It, along with some other terms here, are pathologizing and/or derogatory.

aberration, aestheticism, alternate lifestyle/sexuality/proclivity, amour Socratique, Angelina sorority, Brown family (the), disciple of Oscar Wilde, "diversity," double ribs, gaydom, gay identity, gay lib/liberation, gay lifestyle, gay rights, gaydom, goes to our church, Greek Way (the), gross indecency,

double ribs: an archaic Chinese term for homosexuality
Kinsey Six: the American sexologist Alfred Kinsey described a spectrum of sexual orientation from 1 to 6, 1 being exclusively heterosexual and 6, exclusively homosexual.
Lady-love: a 1930's U.K. term for lesbianism.

> *"All men are capable of homosexual object choice and actually accomplish this in the unconscious."*—Sigmund Freud

in the life, inversion, Kinsey Six, lady-love, lesbianism, LGBTIQQ, love that dares not speak its name (the), nameless crime (the), on the team, one of us, other sex (the), other way (the), pederasty, PLU (people like us), purple power, queer, Roman culture, same sex love, same sex oriented, same sex relations, San Francisco accent (has the), Sapphism, sexual irregularity, sexual orientation, sexual preference, sexual proclivity, sexual tropism, SGL, sugar, third sex (the), LGBTIQQ, unmentionable acts, unmentionable crime, unnatural connection, unnatural crime, unnatural filth, unnatural friendship, unnatural practice, unnatural vice, unspeakable vice, Uranian culture, vice allemande

LGBTIQQ: "Lesbian, gay, bisexual, transgendered, intersexed, queer, and questioning."
"The love that dares not speak its name": coined by Lord Alfred Douglas, Oscar Wilde's lover.
SGL: "Same-gendered loving."

Horny: SEE AROUSED, LUST

Hot: SEE AROUSED, LUST

Hug: SEE CARESS

Hunk: SEE HANDSOME (MALE)

Impotent/Impotence

all show, all talk, no action, anandrious, bad case of the tins, balsa, bent stick, billy-coo, broken machine, bent stick, croopy, crystal dick, dead budgie, dead duck, dead infertile, dead rabbit, dead stick, dead worm, deadwood, dolphin, droop (the), drooping member, droopy/drooper, enfeebled, erectile difficulty/problems, feeble, flaccid, flounder,

Balsam: a semi-erect penis (and soft wood).
Crystal dick: impotence from too many party drugs.
Foster's flop: Australian; impotence induced by too much beer (i.e., Foster's Lager).
Melbourne: a soft, weak hard-on.
Viagra: the impotence medication released in 1998; as a term it is quickly entering the sexual lingo, as well as being the source of many jokes.

Foster's flop, genital failure, half-cocked, Hanging Johnny, have a bent stick, have a broken machine, have stage fright, have brewer's droop, in need of Viagra, incapable, infecund, infertile, infirm, inorgasmic, invirile, limp, limp-dick, mackin', Melbourne, Mr. Softy, muddy waters, no action, no lead in his pencil, no money in his purse/wallet, no toothpaste in the tube, out to pasture, past his prime, performance anxiety, semi-on, sexually dysfunctional, sleeping beast, soft(y), sterile, tulip sauce, useless, Viagra Falls (been to), weak, wet noodle

"His dagger dangled more limply than an unripe beet and never rose to the middle of his tunic."—Catullus, 1st-century B.C.

John: SEE PROSTITUTE'S CLIENT

Kiss (to) SEE ALSO CARESS
"Every time we kiss, we confirm the new world coming"
—Essex Hemphill, gay poet

PHOTO: DIANNE WHELAN

Australian sex, box tonsils, buss, buzz (to), canoodle, cash (a), dutch noodle, exchange spit, face rape, face time (do), French(y), French kiss, give a tonsillectomy, give (one) some sugar, give one the tongue, goo it,

Australian sex: all over kissing and licking the body from up top to "down under." Also: body job.
French kiss: likely derives from un baiser très appuyé, or a kiss heavily

applied.
Mackin': gay surfer term for kissing.
Mwaaah!: the exaggerated sound of an "air-kiss."

"Natalie, my husband kisses your hands, and I the rest"
—Colette, to a lover

grease, grub, have some lip action, have some tongue sushi, hit, lamor, lip, lock lips, lollygag, mack, make kissy-face, make licky-face, make out, make smacky lips, mesh, mouse, mousle, mouth, mouth wrestle, mow, muckle on, mug, muzzle, neck, osculate, PDA, park, pass secrets, peck, perch, plant a big one, plant a kissy-poo, plant a smacker, play kissy, play kissy-poo, play kissy-face, play mouth music, play smacky lips, play tonsil hockey, poof, pucker up, scoop, smack, smooch, smoodge, smoush, snog, snooch, soul kiss, spark, spoon (with), stir, suck face, suck heads, SWAK, swap spit, taste, throw the tongue, tongue wrestle, zoom in

PDA: "Public display of affection."
Smooch: a good example of onomatopoeia in modern slang.
SWAK: "Seal with a kiss."

Labia
SEE ALSO CLITORIS, GENITALIA, VAGINA
From the Latin, labium, for lip. Most of these words were coined by men, but some have been reappropriated by queer women.
Audrey blinds, bacon bomb doors, bacon strips, bacon rind, bag, beef, beef-jibber, blood flaps, bovine drapes, cockles, columns of Venus, cunt lips, curtains, dangly bits, double doors, double suckers, flange, flaps, flesh beer towels, fuck flaps, garden gates, hanging bacon, Hottentot apron, labia majora, labia minora, labs, lips, meat tarp, mince piece, mud flaps, muffin, nether lips, ox drapes, palace gates, passion flaps, pink, pink bits/flaps, piss flaps, portals of sex, sandwich, scallops, sex skin, skins, vaginal rim, vertical bacon (sandwich)

Lesbian
SEE ALSO BUTCH, FEMME, CLOSET CASE
Derives from the Greek isle of Lesbos, where the poet Sappho wrote erotic love verse to women in the 7th century B.C. Sapphic is another adjective for lesbian. Many of these terms are historical and/or homophobic but, in some queer contexts have had their meanings altered.

Amazon, Amy-John, andro-dyke, b-girl, B&D dyke, baby butch, bar trash, bean curd stirrer, baby butch/baby dyke/camper/dinky dyke, bean flicker, bluff, blood spitter, blow sister, boon dagger,

B-girl: a butch lesbian.
Bar trash: a lesbian who trolls bars.
B&D dyke: refers to Black and Decker, a popular line of power tools and suggests a handy gal.
Bean-curd stirrer: the English translation for the Chinese word for lesbian.
Boston marriage: refers to the intensely close relationships between female academics who often lived together.
Clam smacker: 1990s American term for lesbian.
Chicken/baby dyke: a young lesbian.
Clithopper: a loose lesbian.
Cookie duster: a naturally occuring moustache on a lesbian.
CS: "comfortable shoes," code for a potential lesbian sighting.
Cunt positive: a 1970s British term for lesbian.
Demo Dyke: politicized lesbian.

boy, boygul/boygirl, boy dyke, brother, brothergirl, bull, bull bitch, bull dagger, bulldike/dyke, bulldiker/dyker, bumper, butch, butch gal, butchilinity, carpet, carpet muncher, chapstick lesbian, charlie, chicken, chuff muncher, clam smacker, clithopper, closet lez, collar-and-tie, comfortable shoes, cordless massager, crack snaker, crested hen, crack snacker, crunch/crunchies, cunt positive, daddles (one who), daddy, dagger, Demo Dyke, diesel, dike/dyke, DIT, dumptruck, Dy-fu, dykedar, Dykes on Bikes, Dykes on spikes, dykosaurus, dinky, dolly dimple, donut bumper, donut cruncher, drag, duff, dykon, DWOM, earthy-crunchy type, eatalotopus, enforcer, fairy, fairy lady, fanny nosher,

DIT: "Dyke in Training."
Dumptruck: a 1960s U.K. term for a vehicle full of lesbians.
Dyke: like fag or queer in the 20th century; has been reclaimed by queer women and, in queer usage, has become largely devoid of negative connotation, although it originally suggested an excessively masculine woman.

Dykedar: lesbian radar.
Dykes on Bikes: motorcycle-riding lesbians.
Dykes on spikes: lesbian baseball players.

fem(me), female dominator, femme-bo, finger artist, fish bandit, flap cracker, flannel-wearer, fluff, fluzz dyke, frail, frigger, fututrix, fuzz bumper, GAF, gal boy, gal officer, gangster dyke, gangster woman, gap lapper, gash-guzzling gannet, gay chick, gay GAL, GBF, girl jock, girl-lover, girlsloth, girly-girl, glamour dyke, GOF, gold star lesbian, gonsel, goose girl, graceful, granola lesbian, grrrrl, gusset nuzzler, GWF,

PHOTO: DIANNE WHELAN

Fluff/frail/pinky/twist: the passive woman in a lesbian relationship.
GBF: gay black female; GAF/GOF: gay Asian/Oriental female; GWF: gay white female.
Gold star lesbian: a lesbian who has never had sex with a man.

GERTURDE STEIN

gynander, gyngeotrope, hadbian, high diver, horse woman, jasper, ki-ki, king, kissing fish, kitty licker, L, LP, lady lover, lap hugger, lap lover, lapper, leather dyke, leather woman, leg licker, lemon, les, les-be-friends, lesberado, Lesbian Avenger, lesbic, lesbine, lesbo, lesbyterian, leslie, lettie, lettuce licker, lez, lezbo, lezzie, lezzo,

Hadbian: former lesbian.
Kissing Fish: from Monique Lange's 1960 novel of the same name.
L: she put the L in the LPGA (Ladies' Professional Golf Association)!
Lemon/leslie: Australian terms for lesbian.
lesberado: lesbian desperado.

Lilith, lipstick lesbian, little Dutch boy, lover under the lap, low femme, LUG, luppies, major, malflor, mama, man, mantee,

Marge, Mary, Mason, member of the union, minge eater, mintie, mintle, muff diva, muff diver,

Low/medium/high femme: degrees of femininity in dress, appearance.
LP: "Lesbian Potential."
LUG: "Lesbian until graduation (from college)."
Luppies: lesbian yuppies.
Mama: a feminine lesbian.
Mantee: from French mante *for praying mantis—a very masculine, if not predatory lesbian.*
Palone omee: Polari for lesbian.
Pancake: a butch lesbian who allows herself to be a bottom.
Power lesbian: an A-list gal.
PL: "Professional lesbian." Also: Luppie.
Running shoe lesbian: A casually-dressed lesbian who favours sneakers.

Nelly, nymphette, omelette maker, on the other bus, one who is in a Boston marriage, other sex (the), PC dyke (politically correct), palone omee, pancake, pansy without a stem, pap, pinky, PL, plate-licker, poppa, pot, potential, power dyke, power lesbian, puss, queen, queer queen, rag doctor, Raleigh bike, rooster, ruffle, running shoe lesbian, rug muncher, Santa Fe (someone who goes to), sapphic love, sapphist, Saturday Night Butch, screwball, sergeant, sensible shoes-wearer, she-male, she-man, slack, slacks, slut puppy, soft butch, Special K, spinster, split tail lover, stone, stone butch, sucker, sushi, sushi lover, sulley, tennis fan, tennis player, thespian, third sex (the), third sexer, three-wheeler, tit-king, Tom, tomboy, tootsie, top sergeant, tortillera, tribadist, truck driver, tuna face, tuppence lapper, tuppence lick-

PHOTO: DIANNE WHELAN

er, twinky, twist, vagitarian, vegetable, velcro, vulva hands, wannabe, wolf, woman-loving-woman (WLW), womon, Xena-lover, yessir, zamie, zamie girl

To go to Santa Fe: a U.S. expression from the 1920s-30s describing a woman "who had switched her sexuality."
Saturday Night Butch: butch on weekends only.
Special K: a lesbian priest.
Sushi: Asian lesbian.
Potboiler novels in the 1950s frequently made reference on their covers to the "third sex" or the "other sex," to titillate mostly male readers.
Womon/womyn/wimmin: lesbian and feminist spellings which remove "man" or "men" from references to females.
Zamie/zamie girl: a West Indian term for lesbian.

> "Went out last night,
> With a crowd of my friends,
> They must be womens
> 'Cause I don't like mens"
> —Ma Rainey

Lesbian Sex

SEE CUNNILINGUS, MASTURBATION, ORAL SEX

bumper to bumper, clam jousting, clit fight, daddle, diddle, donut to donut, dyking out, finger-fuck, fuck, frig, fottage, giv'r, going down there, hump, lezzing out, make scissors, processing, rub, rubbing muff, rubbing mirrors, tribadism, twat lapping, velcro fastening

Daddle: to enjoy lesbian sex.
Feminate (to): a term for lesbian sex.
Make scissors: refers to a sexual position for clit-on-clit action.
Processing: sarcastic reference to the often lengthy negotiations lesbians put their new partners through before they will "get physical."
Rubbing mirrors: Chinese expression for tribadism, involves the rubbing of one clit against the other.
Dry date/dry fuck/dry hump/dry rub/dry run: frottage.

Lick

SEE ALSO BITING, MOUTH, KISSING, SWALLOWING, ORAL SEX.

The tongue is most definitely a sexual organ.

flick(er), lap, mouth job, mouth, mouth-wash, slobber, slurp, suck, taste, tongue, tongue bath, tongue job, tongue-fuck

lip-flick: a subtle toungue wagging used as a sign of interest when cruising.

Love (to)

SEE ALSO DESIRE (TO)

It's surprising that relatively few slang terms for love, either gay or straight, exist when compared to sexual practices or body parts.

admire, adore, after (be), all up in someone (be), attached to (be), bitten (be), cherish, crazy about (be), crazy for (be), cuckoo over (be), dead set on (be), delight in, desire, devoted (be), enchanted by (be), fall for, fancy, fascinated by (be), fond of (be), go for, gone on (be), gooey about (be), gooey over (be), goofy about (be),

groove on, gushy (be), have a crush, have a pash for, have a passion for, have a ring through your nose, have a sweet tooth for, have a thing for, have a yearning for, have affection for, have ardour for, have esteem for, have eyes for, have fervor, have fond-ness for, have the hots for, have it bad, have loyalty for, have your nose open, have passion for, head over heels (be), hold in high esteem, hold in high regard, idealize, idolize, in a bad way (be), in deep (be), infatuated with (be), like, long for, look of love (the), lose your heart to, lovey-dovey (to be), lust for, mad about (be), moony over (be), mushy (be), nuts about (be), on a tight leash (be), pash, pine for, prize, put on pedestal, really like, rush, shook on (be), slushy (be), smitten (be), snowed over (be), soft on (be), sprung on (be), stuck on, struck by lightning (be), sweet on (be), take a shine to, taken with, think everything of, think the world of, treasure, wear the ring, wild about (be), wild for (be), worship, yearn for, zealous (be)

Have the hots for: an American term from the mid-20th century; describes the heat of passion.

"The look of love is in your eyes. . ."
—"The Look of Love," Burt Bacharach, 1967

Lust

SEE ALSO AROUSED

amativeness, amour, ardour, arousal, bad intentions, burn, carnal sin, carnality, concupiscence, craving, desire, desires of the flesh, eroticism, fire in the balls, horniness, hot pants, hots (the), impure thoughts, itch, lustfulness, nasties (the), nasty thoughts, nature, old Adam (the), passion, pride, prurience, sexual appetite, sin of passion, sinful thoughts, sins of the flesh, urge to merge (the), weakness of the flesh, wicked thoughts, wickedness, yen-yen

"Men, leaving the natural use of the woman, burned in their lust toward one another"—Romans 1:26 (The Bible)

Masturbation

The "hidden vice" is no longer hidden, as this rather lengthy list reveals.

abuse, arm breaker, auto pilot, bachelor's delight, bananas and cream, Barclay's Bank, beastliness, biff ball, blanket drill, bluevein shuffle, cheesy rollback, chicken-milking, cunt-cuddling, devil's handshake, dicky-whacking, diddling, dildo-doodling, DIY, dong flogging, fetch mettle, finger painting,

Barclay's Bank: a British example of rhyming sexual slang (i.e., wank).
DIY: "Do it yourself."

finger fuck, five against one, five-finger Mary, four sisters on Thumb Street, frigging, genital sensate focusing, gherkin-jerking, grind grip, gusset typing, ham-boning, hand-gallop, hand-jive, hand-job, hand-shandy, handle, hot rod, infanticide, j/o scene, Jodrell Bank, knob job, Levy and Frank, MM/M&M, manual exercise, manual job, manual pollution, menage à un, Mother Fist and her five daughters, Mr. Hand, motherfish, Onan's Olympics, onanism, one stick from improvisation, one-legged race, one-off the wrist, pink piston practice, playing chopsticks, pocket job, pocket pool, pollution, Portuguese pump(ing), pull yourself, pulling the goalie, rod-walloping, secret sin, secret vice, self-abuse, self-pleasuring, self-pollution, short strokes, shower spank, simple infanticide, slaking the bacon, soldier's joy, solitary sin, spank(ing), tap dancing, twatty wank, Uncle Frank, wakey, wakey, hands of snakey, wanking, white-water wristing, whizzing the jizzum, wrist aerobics, wrist job, yankee

MM/M&M: mutual masturbation (and the extent of some gay men's sexual activity).
Pulling the goalie: a Canadian, hockey-inspired euphemism.

Masturbate (to) (Female)
These terms are examples of 20th-century slang invented almost exclusively by women.
air the orchid, apply lip gloss, baste the tuna, beat your beaver, brush your beaver, bury your knuckles, buff the weasel, butter your muffin, buttonhole, caress your kitty, catch a buzz, clap your clit, clap with one hand, clean your fur coat, clout your cookie, club the clam, cook cucumbers, digitate, do your nails, do something for your chapped lips, drill for oil, dunk the beaver, express yourself, fan your fur, feed your fish, feed your horse, finger paint, finger-fuck, flick off, flit your clit, frig, floss the cat, fondle the fig, get a date with slick mittens, get a fat lip, get a lube job, get a stain out of your carpet, glaze the donut, go it alone, grab your goatee, grease your gash, grease your skillet,

grease your lips, hand shandy, hit the slit, hitchhike to heaven, hose your hole, hula-hoop, itch your ditch, jill off, leglock the pillow, lick your lips, light the candle, lube the tube, lube your labia, make your kitty purr, make your pussy purr, make waves, massage your clit, mistressbate, paddle the pink canoe, part the Red Sea,

Jill off: the female equivalent of jacking off, as in "Jack and Jill went up the hill."
Mistressbate: takes away reference to the master in this female pastime.

pat your snatch, perm the poodle, pet Snoopy, pet your poodle, pet your pussy, play couch hockey for one, play stinky pinky, play with the little man in the boat, poke the pucker, poke your pussy, polish your peanut, preheat the oven, read Braille, ring for the maid, rub job, rub off, rub your hubbin, scratch your patch, self-pleasure, self-love, self-manipulate, she-bop, shuck your oyster, slam your clam,  Southern Comfort (a bit of), stir your yoghurt, stump-jump, surf the channel, surf the wet, take a dip, take a trip to the deep South, test the plumbing, thumb, thumb your button, tickle your crack, tickle your fanny, tickle your tack, twit your clit, twit your slit, type at the gusset, use a vibrator, visit Father Fingers, walk the hand home, water the hot spot, wax the candlestick, wax the womb, work in the garden

"She-Bop" was a pop hit for Cyndi Lauper in 1984.

Masturbate (to) (Male)

abuse yourself, address congress, Anne Frank (to), Arthur (to), audition the finger puppets, ball off, bang the banjo, bash your bishop, bat, beat, beat it, beat off, beat your dummy, beat your hog, beat your little brother, beat your meat, beat your bishop, beat your pup, blanket drill (the), blooch, bludgeon your beefsteak, bob, boff, bop, bop your baloney, box the Jesuit, box the Jesuit and get cockroaches, brandle, bring down by hand, bring yourself off, buff your helmet, buff your pylon, burp your baby, burp your woman, burp your work, butter your corn, call for more mayo, catch a buzz,

Anne Frank: rhymes with wank.
Catch a buzz: to masturbate with a vibrator.

charm your snake, choke your chicken, choke your chook, choke your gopher, chuff, churn your butter, circle jerk (in a group), clean your rifle, climb Mount Baldy, clutch the bear, coax your cojones, come your mutton, come your turkey, consult Dr. Jerkoff, corral your tadpoles, crack your nuts, crank your shank, crimp your wire, cuff your governor, cuff your meat, dash your doodle, diddle, digitate, dinky your slinky, do a dry waltz with yourself, do it yourself, do yourself off, do paw-paw tricks, do some handy work, do the dildo thing, do the five-finger knuckle shuffle, dong flogging, eat cockroaches, faire zague-zague, fax the pope, feel in your pocket for your big hairy rocket, fetch mettle, fight your turkey, file your fun-rod, finger, finger-fuck, fist-fuck, fist your mister, five against one, five knuckle chuckle (do the), flex your sex, flick your Bic, flip yourself off, flog, flog your bishop, flog your dog, flog your dolphin, flog your dong, flog your donkey, flog your dong, flog your dummy, flog your frog, flog your log, flog your meat, flog your mutton, flog your sausage, flog yourself, fluff your duff, fondle your fig, frig, frig yourself, friggle, fuck off, fuck your fist, fuck yourself, gallop the antelope, gallop the lizard, gallop the maggot, get a grip on things, get a hold of yourself, get cockroaches, get your nuts off, gherkin-jerking, give a one-gun salute, go it alone, gong your dong, grease your pipe, grind, grip, grip it, grip your pencil, grow hairs on your palms, hack your mack, hand jive, handle, handle yourself, haul your own ashes, have a salty handshake, have a tug, hold a bowling ball, hone your cone, hop your balcony, hump your hose, husk, husker, j/o, jack off, jack your beanstalk, jag off, jazz yourself, jell off, jerk, jerk off, jerk your gherkin, jerk your mutton,

Five against one: refers to five fingers grabbing the solitary member.
Jack off: an American expression for masturbation, deriving from jack, one of the synonyms for both penis and semen.
Kinky your slinky: an example of humorous rhyming, extremely common in sexual slang through the ages.

ATTRIB. LATTIMER, U.S., C. 1940.
THOMAS WAUGH COLLECTION

jerk your turkey, jerker, jive, keep the census down, keep the population down, kinky your slinky, knob, lark, Levy, lube your tube, magazine date (have a), make the bald man cry, make the scene, man the cockpit, manipulate your mango, manipulate your member, manual exercise, manual pollution, manustupration, married to Mary, massage your muscle, milk your chicken, milk your lizard, milkman (be a), mitten queen, mount a corporal and four, oil your glove, pack your palm, paddle your pickle, paint your ceiling, paw-paw tricks, phone the czar, pickle-paddling, play a flute solo on your meat whistle, play off, play pocket billiards, play solitaire, play your organ, play with yourself, please your pisser, plunk your twanger, point your social finger, pole vault, polish your rocket, polish your sword,

Play pocket pool: refers to self-fondling through trouser pockets.
Punish Percy in the palm: an example of alliterative sexual slang.

polish your china, pollute, pollution, pommel the priest, Portuguese pump, pound off, pound your flounder, pound your meat, pound your peenie, pound your pomegranate, pound your pork, pound your pud, prime your pump, prod the peepee, prompt your porpoise, prune the fifth limb, pull about, pull off, pull your joint, pull your peter, pull your pud, pull your pudding, pull your taffy, pull your wire, pull yourself off, pull your goalie, pull your pope, pull wire, pump off, pump your pickle, pump your python, pump your stump, punish Percy in the palm, ram the ham, reach around, romance your bone, rub, rub off, rub up, run your hand up the flagpole, rub your genie, screw off, secret handshake, self-abuse, self-pollution, sew, shag, shag off, shake, shake your snake, shake up, she-bop, shine your pole, shoot your tadpoles, shuck your corn, slake your bacon, slam your hammer, slam your spam, slam your salami, slap your wrapper, sling your jelly, sling your juice, snake it, snap the rubber, snap your twig, snap your whip, soldier's joy, spank (yourself), spank your Frank, spank your monkey, spank your salami, spank your wife's best friend, spill your seed,

Self-pollution: derived from the 17th century and makes reference to historical assumptions that masturbation was both immoral and physically detrimental or defiling.
To wank: used at least since the 1800s; may represent a joining of yank *and* whack*, other common euphemisms for masturbation.*

squeeze off, squeeze your cheese, squeeze your lemon, stir your stew, strike the pink match, stroke (yourself), stroke your beef, stroke your bloke, stroke your dog, stroke your lizard, stroke your poker, strum the old Banjo, take down, take yourself in hand, talk with Rosy Palm and her five little sisters, tantalize your tassel, tame your shrew, tap dance,

ANON., U.S., c. 1940s.
THOMAS WAUGH COLLECTION.

tease your weasel, throttle Kojak, thump your pumper, tickle your ivory, tickle your pickle, toss off, toss your salad, touch up, tug your tubesteak, twang your wire, tweak your twinkle, unclog your pipes, varnish your pole, visit the five-fingered fiend, walk your dog, waltz with Willy, wank, wank off, waste time, watch the eyelid movies, wax your dolphin, whack off, whack your bishop, whang off, whank, whank off, whip it, whip off, whip your dripper, whip your dummy, whizz your jism, whip your wire, wonk your conker, work it off, work off, wrench off, wrestle your eel, yang your wang, yank, yank off, yank your crank, yank your plank, yank your strap, yank your yam

Masturbator
candlestick-polisher, chicken-choker, christian, diddler, dink-rubber, Gavin, hog-flogger, jerk, jerk-off, jerk-off addict, mega-wanker, Merchant banker, milkman, mitten queen, onanist, peter-beater, Portnoy, pud-puller, solo-sexual, stroker, tosser, tube-stroker, wank bandit, wanker

Mitten queen: a gay man fond of wanking.

Menage à Trois
SEE ALSO ORGY
club sandwich, cluster fuck, double adapter, double peptide, lucky Pierre, menage a toits, Oreo cookie, sandwich, sausage sandwich, spit-roasting, three-hole activities, three-in-a-bed, three-way, threesome triangle of love, two plus one,

Oreo cookie: a threesome between two black persons and one white.
Sausage sandwich: three men layered just so.

Menstrual Pad/Tampon
SEE ALSO MENSTRUATION, TO MENSTRUATE
ammunition, bandage, birdy, clout, cork, cotton pony, cover, cur-

tain, diaper, do rag, fanny rag, feminine protection, flag, G-string, granny rag, hammock, jam rag, jelly sandwich, Keeper (the), Kotex, labia landfill, launching pad, little white mouse, Luna Pads, manhole cover, menstrual cloth, minge mouse, monthly rag, napkin, O.B., pad, panty liner, perineal pad, pleasure-garden padlock,

The Keeper: A reusable rubber cup, inserted vaginally to collect menstrual fluid.
Luna Pads: Available in health food stores, these cloth pads are washable and come in stylish prints including leopard and tiger. They are to tampons as a pencil to a futon.
O.B., Kotex, and Tampax are among many brand name products.
Rag: 20th-century American term; a piece of cloth to absorb blood during menses (on the rag).
Tampon: from the verb tamp, *or to block a hole.*

plug, poe-slap, pon, Prince Charlie, protection, rag, red rag, sanitary, sanitary pad, sanitary towel/st, shoe, slingshot, Tampax, tampon, twat hammock, window blind, window curtain

Menstrual Period

SEE ALSO MENSTRUATE (TO), MENSTRUAL PAD/TAMPON

Euphemisms for menstruation are an example of slang invented almost entirely by women. Until the 20th century, most "dirty words" were formulated by boys and men.

Arsenal's playing at home, Aunt Flo, bad news, bad week, Baker flying, bends (the), bellringer, beno, blob, blodded park, Bloody Mary, bubbled up, carrying the flag, catamenia, catamenial discharge, catamenial state, chinkerings, clit clot, collywobbles, coming on, country cousin, courses, curse, curse of Eve, das, dog days,

DAs: "Domestic afflictions."
Dysmenorrhea: painful periods.

domestic afflictions, dysmenorrhea, female disorder, female

trouble, feminine matters, field day, flag day, flagging, floods, flowers, flowing, flux, flying Baker, flying the flag, flying the Japanese flag, flying the red flag, friends to stay, full of one's bike, grandmother, gym queen, hammock is swinging, hell week, high tide, holy week, ill, immenses, indisposed, irregular periods, little friend, little sister, little visitor,

Female Trouble *was the name of a 1975 film by John Waters and starring the legendary Divine.*
Menses: Latin for monthly.
Moontime: New-Age expression borrowing from the First Nations' association of menstruation and moon cycles.
OTR (on the rag) and TTOM (that time of the month): examples of short-hand used among women to make discreet reference to menstruation.

menses, menstrual period, minge week, monthlies, monthly bill, monthly blues, monthly causes, monthly cycle, monthly flowers, monthly flux, monthly period, monthly rag, monthly term, months, moontime, mother nature, muscle queen, nature, nuisance (the), off the roof, off limits, on the blob, on the rag/OTR, out of order, period, rag time, ragging, really slick, red dog on a white horse, red flag, red Mary, red rag, red sails in the sunset, red tummy ache, red-haired visitor (the), regular periods, riding the cotton pony, riding the rag, road making, road up for repairs, roses, sick, so, squirting clots, steroid queen, stomach cramps, stormy weather, tail flowers, Tampax time, terms, that time, that way, thing (the), those days of the month/TTOM, tummy ache, tums, turns, twitters, vapours, visit from Flo, visitor, visitor with red hair, wallflower week, wet season, woman's home companion, women's things, wrong time of the month

Menstruate (to)
SEE ALSO MENSTRUATION, SANITARY NAPKIN
Men have perhaps tended to be rather mystified by female bodily cycles and use very few of these terms.
become a lady, bloody flag is up (the), captain is home (the), car-

dinal is home (the), Charlie's come, entertain the general, fall off the roof, feel poorly, feel unwell, flag is out, flag is up, flash the red flag, fly the flag, fly the red flag, got the rag on, got menstruation, have a caller, have a little visitor, have it on, have your aunt, have your friend, have your granny, have the bends, have the flag out, have the flowers, have the painters in, have the rag on, indisposed, kit has come, on the rag (be), on the saddle (be), your captain has come, your friend has come, on the rag/otr, painters/decorators are in, put the flags out, raggin', Red army in town, Red Sea (be in the), ride the rag, ride the red house, see your aunt, see your auntie, see your friend, start bleeding, stay (to), stub your toe, under the weather (be), unwell (be)

Monogamy/Monogamous

SEE ALSO PROMISCUOUS MALE/FEMALE, CASUAL SEX PARTNER

Some gay liberationists argue that our ability to have monogamous gay relationships demonstrates we are natural and normal. Others say that promiscuity and polyamoury are the gay birthright.

batch night, exclusive, fusion, hitched, living the het love fantasy, LTR, married, monotony, off limits, serial monogamist, significant other

Batch night: a designated evening for LTRs to go cruising seperately, a night off from monogamy.
LTR: "long-term relationship."

Mouth

aperture, bazoo, beak, BJL, box, cake-hole, chops, clam, cock-holster, crevice, face-hole, face-pussy, fag-hole, fish trap, flapper, funnel, gabber, gap, gob, hatch, hot lips, kisser, kissing trap, lips, mush, north and south, orifice, puss, rubies, smacker, smush, talk trap, trap, yapper

BJL: "Blow job lips."
Rubies: lips.

Muscular/A Muscular Man

SEE ALSO HANDSOME (MALE), CHEST

This expanding list suggests a growing societal preoccupation with male appearance and physique.

Adonis, animal, argonaut, athletic, BB, beefaroni, big, big boy, blowfish, boxed, brawny, broad-shouldered, bruiser, bruising, bubbled up, buff(ed), built, built like a brick shithouse, bulstrode, burly, chiseled, Clark Kent, cock diesel, compact, cut, defined, discotits, diesel, float, firm, forceful, giant, God (a), god-like, guns, gym bot, gym bunny, gym queen, hard-assed, heifers,

BB: "Body builder."
Clark Kent: a well-dressed, muscular man.
Guns, pythons: body builders' references to big arms.
Heifers: large calf muscles.

TONY SANSONE BY EDWIN F. TOWNSEND, U.S., C. 1932.
THOMAS WAUGH COLLECTION

hefty, Herculean, hoss, hot bod, huge, hulking, hulky, humpy, humongous, hungry, hunky, husky, industrial, iron pumper, iron man, lean, leanard, macho man, mammoth, man-sized, mean, meathead, mighty, mighty powerful, Mr. Man, muscle boy, muscle muffin, muscleman, muscle Mary, muscle worshipper, musclehead, muscly, Neanderthal, on juice, puffed out, pumped,

On juice: using steriods.
Ripped: refers to the shredded or cut appearance of well-defined muscles.

pumped-up, pythons, ripped, rock-hard, rock-like, roid master, shoulders out-to-here, sinewy, solid, sporty, stacked, stalwart, statuesque, steroid-enhanced, strapping, strong, strong-arm, studly, sturdy, superjock, thick, thickset, tight body/bod, toned, tough, uman, V-shaped, vascular, well put together, well-built, well-constructed, well-defined, well-made, wiry, yoked

Vascular: refers to the sometimes dramatic appearance of veins on bodybuilders. This is often achieved through use of fluid restriction or diuretics.

Nipples

buds of beauty, buttons, champagne corks, cherries, cherrylets, coat hangers, dinners, dockyard rivets, dubs, dugs, eyes, kitten's noses, knobs, M&M's, mammae, nibbles, niblets, ninnies, nipplefest, nipply-do-dahs, nips, nubs, num-nums, nums, pap heads, papilla mamae, paps, piggies, points, pup- pies raspberries, raspberry ripple, rosebuds, smarties, strawberries, teats, thumbtacks, tits, Tune in, Tokyo

Tune in, Tokyo: nipple twisting.

Nude

Always in flux, the current attitude toward nudity and the display of the body is quite relaxed, as the obvious humour in many of these terms demonstrate.

ANON. C. 1930s.
THOMAS WAUGH COLLECTION

Adam (like), Adamatical, Adam's PJ's, all face, as God made him, au naturel, ballock naked, ballocky, bare, bare naked, bare-assed, bareskin, bareass, barepoles, belly naked, birth naked, birthday attire, bleat, blete, body naked, bollock naked, bollocky starkers, buck naked, buff, buff bare, buffo, butt naked, disrobed, frontal nudity, full frontal, full monty, garb of Eden, go-buttons, Harry Starkers, in a natural state, in a state of nature, in cuerpo, in Morocco, in your birthday suit, in puris naturalibus, in stag, in the altogether, in the buff, in the natural, in the noddle, in the noodie, in the nuddie, in the nuddy, in the nude, in the raw, in the rude, Lady Godiva, laid to the natural bone, mother naked, naked, naked as a jaybird, naked buff, native buff, nature's garb (in), necked, nuddy, on the shallows, peeled, practice nudism, raw, skuddy, starbollock naked, starbolic naked, stark, stark ballux, stark bone naked,

PHOTO: DIANNE WHELAN

Birthday suit: dates to the 16th century, referring to being born naked.
Lady Godiva: nickname for a gay man who lounges in his house naked.
Stark: as in stark naked; may derive from stert, meaning tail.

stark born naked, stark mother naked, stark naked, stark-bullock naked, starkers, starko, stripped, unclad, unclothed, uncovered, undraped, undressed, wearing a birthday suit, wearing a smile, wearing nothing but a smile, wearing your Sunday suit, wholly naked, without a stitch

Oral Sex (General)

SEE ALSO CUNNILINGUS, FELLATIO

blow job, bob, eating someone out, fork and spoon, Frenching, gamming, giving head, giving lip service, gob job, going down and doing tricks, going down for the gravy, going down on someone, going downtown, gobble someone, gummer, head date, head job, kneeling at the altar, Lewinsky, licking, loop-the-loop, lunch, making an O,

Giving head: a 20th-century expression deriving from the fact that oral sex is done with the head on a head (the glans of the penis).
Okawa: French-Canadian slang for blow job.

making mouth music, noshing, oral-genital sex/intimacy, oral intercourse, picnic, plating someone, rubbernecking, scarfing down, scarfing up, scoffing, servicing orally, sixty-nine, skull job, sodomy, soixante-neuf, speaking low, speaking genitalese, talking turkey, tongue, tricking off, trim

"I regret to say that we of the FBI are powerless to act in cases of oral-genital intimacy, unless it has some way obstructed interstate commerce."—J. Edgar Hoover

Orgasm (to Achieve)

SEE ALSO EJACULATE

The predominance of male-derived terms in this list seems to suggest that the female orgasm is a modern invention.

Blast off, bring off, bust off, cheer, cheese, climax, come/cum, come off, come your cocoa, come your fat, convulse, cream, cream your jeans, cream your silkies, deposit, die, discharge, dry, ejaculate, emission, fade, fall in the furrow, fanny bomb, FBO, fire, get off, get your balls off, get your gun off, get your nuts off, get your rocks off, go over the mountain, have a double shot, have a nocturnal, have a small stroke, have a wet dream, have your ticket punched,

"To come" was used in Shakespeare's time to refer to achieving orgasm but remains a popular euphemism today.
FBO: "Full body orgasm."
Fanny bomb: a female orgasm.

hit the top, jet your juice, light off, little death, love come down, melt, number three, peak, pleasure, pop, pop your cookie, pop your cork, pop your nuts, say yes!, see stars, shake and shiver, shoot off your load, shoot your load, shoot your roe, shoot your wad, spend, spew, spit, squirt, stand up and shout, stand upward, take your pleasure, thrill, throw up

Religious invocations are common phrases uttered by men and women as they climax: "Oh my God," "Oh God," "Oh Jesus."

Orgy

SEE ALSO MENAGE À TROIS

As we all know, orgies are not a new phenomenon. The terminology used in referring to them is often humourous, as this list reveals.

all in one, American trombone, back up, bareback party, bender, bigynist (two women), birthday party, buff ball, buffet flat, Buffet flat, bunch punch, chain gang, chain jerk, choo choo,

Bareback party: an orgy without condoms.
Buffet flat, chain gang, cockfest, daisy chain, floral arrangement, pig pile, poke party, and Roman night all refer to gay orgies.
Fourgy/foursome/fourway: a four-person orgy.

chugga chugga, circle jerk, circus, circus love, club sandwich, cluster fuck, cluster marriage, cockfest, daisy chain, everythingathon, festival, fet party (fetish), flesh picnic, floral arrangement, fourgy, foursome, fourway, fuck-a-rama, fuckathon, gang ball, gang bang, gang shag, gang shay, grabathon, grope-in, group grope, group sex, Jack-and-Jill-a-thon, Jack-and-Jill-off, key swap, line up on, Marty-machlia, Mazola party, menage à trois, milkrace, moresome, mutual masturbation, oil party, par-tay, party, petting party, picnic, pig pile, poke party, pulling a train, pull party, ring around the rosy, ring jerk, Roman historian, Roman night, Roman party, round pound, round robin, running a double train, Russian salad party, sandwich,

Mazola party: 20th-century; refers to a brand-name vegetable oil used for massage and lubrication in sex parties (variations: oil party, Wesson party).
Milkrace: a circle jerk.
Roman historian: someone who likes orgies.

Skeeze: African-American for engaging in an orgy.

sewing circle, sex marathon, skeeze, sloppy seconds, spit roast, suckathon, swing party, swinging, team cream, team play, team sport, three-way, three-way deal, threesome, triangle, turn out, ultimate (the), vanilla and chocolate, Wesson party

> *"Home is heaven and orgies are vile/ But you need an orgy, once in a while"*
> —*Ogden Nash*

Penetrate (to)

SEE ALSO SODOMIZE, LESBIAN SEX

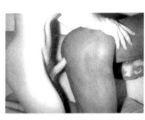

JOHN BARRINGTON, U.K., C. 1969.
THOMAS WAUGH COLLECTION

bore, break and enter (B&E), dig, dilate, drill, drive, drive into, enter, finger, force, force into, hammer, impale, impregnate, insert, invade, jab, lance, nail, needle, open, pack (to), packing, peel (open), perloste, pierce, plow, plunge, plunge into, poke, pound, prick, probe, prod, pry open, puncture, put to, ream, rip, rupture, shread, skewer, slam, slam-bam, slash, slit, spear, spike, spread, stab, stick (into), tear, thrust, whack

Packing/pack (to): to wear a strap-on dildo.
Poke: as in jab, prod, penetrate: dates back to the 18th century.
Big J: simultaneously fucking and blowing your partner: requires good flexibility.

Penis

SEE ALSO ERECTION, GLANS, GENITALIA (MALE), TESTICLES, WELL-ENDOWED

This list does not include the countless terms of endearment individual grown men give to their members. One example is a Montreal man who called his penis Scouty because it was "always up and ready," just like a boy scout. This list wins prize for the largest number of synonyms. No word in any language has as many synonyms as the word penis in English. Men have always been preoccupied by their members

and their language certainly reflects this.
3-4-2-5, Aaron's rod, Abraham, acorn, affair, agate, all forlorn, almard, almond, almond rock, angle, anteater, arborvitae,

3-4-2-5: spells dick on a telephone dial.
Agate: a small penis.
Bald-headed hermit: refers both to penis and the glans.
Bagaga: Polari for penis.

arm, arrow, ass-opener, ass-wedge, auld hornie, baby, bagaga, bagpipes, bald-headed candidate, bald man, bald-headed hermit, bald-headed mouse, baloney, baloney pony, banana, banger, bar, bat, battering piece, battering ram, bauble, bayonet, bazooka, beak, bean, bean-tosser, beef, beef bayonet, bed-muscle, bell-end, bell-rope, belly, belly ruffian, best friend, best leg of three, Bethlehem steel, between the legs, bicho, big bird, big brother, big clit, big daddy, big foot Joe, big one, big piece of meat, Big Steve, big wand, bilbo, bingy, bird, bishop, bitte, blackjack, blacksnake, blade, blood-breaker, blow-stick, blow-torch, bludgeon, blue-vein, blue-veined custard chucker, blue-veined hooligan/BVH, blue-veined piccolo, blueskin, blunt end, bob tail, bodkin, bocack, bo-jack, bon bon, bone, bonfire, bow, bowsprit, box, boy, boycock, boy's delight, bracmard, broom handle, broomstick, bug-fucker, bugle, bum-tickler, burrito, burrow, bush-beater, bush-whacker, busk, butter-knife, button-hole worker, cadulix, callibistris, canary, candle, candy stick, cane, cannon, Captain Picard, capullito, cark, carnal stump, carrot, cartsz/o, Cecil, chanticleer, charger, Charlie, cherry-picker, cherry-splitter, chicken, child-getter, chingus, chink-stopper, chitterling, choad, chooza, chopper, chorizo, chull, chum, clava, clothes prop, club, CO (cock odour), cobra, crowbar, cock, cock of death, cockmeat, cockshaft, cod, colleen bawn, copperstick, coral branch,

Cartes/cartzo: Polari for penis.
Captain Picard: the bald-headed leader on TV's Star Trek: The Next Generation.

Cock: used since the 17th century; may derive from rooster or watercock: i.e., faucet spout.
Cyclops: not unlike "one-eyed monster."

corey, corncob, crack-hunter, cracksman, crank, cranny-hunter, creamstick, crimson, crimson chitterling, crook, crotch cobra, crowbar, crumpet trumpet, cuckoo, cucumber, culty gun, cunt-stabber, custard chucker, cutlass, Cyclops, daddy, dagger, dang, dangle-dong, dangler, dangling participle, dark meat, dart, dart of love, dearest member, derrick, devil, dibble, dick, dickory dock, dickshaft, dicky,

Dark meat: a black man's penis.
Dick: in the 1890s, there was a notorious hangman in London named Derrick. Dying prisoners in Derrick's noose sometimes developed an erection apparently referred to as a Derrick, a term later shortened to Dick.

diddle, dildo, dimple-dick, ding-a-ling, ding-dong, dingbat, dinger, dinghy, dingle, dingle-dangle, dingus, dingus diving rod, dink, dinosaur, dipstick, dirk, ditty, divining rod, do-jigger,

"My Ding-a-Ling" was a number one hit for Chuck Berry in 1972.

Doc(tor) Johnson, dofunny, dog, dohicky, dohinger, dojigger, dojohnnie, dolly, dong(er), donkey, donkey-rigged, doo-flicker, doodle, doohickey, doover, doowhackey, dork, down-leg, dragon, dribbling dart of love, driving post, dropping member, drum-stick, ducky-bird, ducy, dummy, dydus, eel, eggwhite cannon, eikel, eleventh finger, end, enemy, engine, enob, equipment, eye-opener, fag, family organ, fanny ferret, fat peter, father-confessor, ferret, fiddle-bow, firebrand, fish, fishing rod, flaccid prick, flap-doodle, flapper, flip-flop, floater, flute, foaming beef probe, fool-sticker, foot, foreman, fornicating engine, fornicating member, fornicating tool, fornicator, four-eleven-forty-four, frankfurter, friend, frigamajig, Fritz, fuck-stick, fuck tool, fucker, fuckpole, fuckprong, fun-stick, gadget, gadso,

Enob: bone *spelled backwards.*

Four-eleven-forty-four: refers to the purported average size of a black man's penis: four inches around, eleven inches in length. An example of ethnic stereotyping in sexual slang.

gap-stopper, garden engine, gardener, gaying instrument, gearstick d'amour, generation tool, gentle tittler, German helmet, gherkin, gigglestick, giggling pin, Giorgio, girlometer, gladius, glans, goober, good time, goose's neck, gooser, goot, gourd, gravy-giver, gravy-maker, green-coloured dick, grinding tool, gristle, gristle-stick, guided missile, gully-raker, gun, gun hair-splitter, gutstick, hacker, hair-divider, hair-splitter, half a cob, hambone, hammer, hampton, Hampton rock, Hampton Wick,

ANON. U.S., c. 1950s.
THOMAS WAUGH COLLECTION

handle, handstaff, hanging Johnny, hard-on, Harry, He Who Must Be Obeyed, helmet, hermit, hickey, hoe-handle, hog, holy poker, honeypot cleaver, honk(er), hootchee, horn, horn hose, horse cock, hose, hotrod, humpmobile, hung, hunk of meat, hunky, ibm, ice cream machine, id, idol, implement, impudence,

Gherkin: yet another food metaphor. See also pickle, kosher pickle.
IBM: "Itty bitty meat"; refers to a small penis.
Irish root: an English expression for penis; Irish toothache *is an erection. Both are examples of rather benign ethnic attribution in erotic slang.*

inch instrument, instrument, intimate part, intimate person, Irish root, it, jack, Jack Robinson, jack-in-the-box, Jacob, Jacques,

Jacques' jammy, jammy, jang, jargonelle, Jean-Claude, jelly-bean, jemmison, jemson, jerking-iron, Jezebel, jig jigger, jiggle bone, jiggling bone, Jimbo, jimmy, jing-jang, jock, jockam/ jockum/jocum, jocky, Johhnie, John, John Thomas, John Willie, Johnson, joing, joint, jolly roger, Jones, jongeheer, joy knob, joy prong, joy stick, Julius Caesar, junior, justum, key, kidney-scraper, kidney-wiper, king-member, knob, knobster, knock(er), kosher, kosher pickle, labourer of nature, lad (the), lamp of fire, lance, lance of love, langolee, lanyard, larydoodle, licorice stick, life-preserver, lifeless, lingam, little brother, Little Davy, little dick, Little Elvis, little finger, little friend, little man, little peter, little pinkie, little sliver of flesh, little stick, little wiener, Little Willie, little worm, live rabbit, live sausage, liver-turner, lizard, lob, lob-cock, lobster, log, lollypop, long John, long Tom, long-arm inspection, love dart, love gun, love luger, love machine, love muscle, love pump, love sausage, love steak,

Little Elvis: what Elvis Presley allegedly called his love muscle.
"I'm just a love machine, And I won't work for nobody but you."
—The Miracles' disco hit, "Love Machine," 1975

love stick, love tool, love torpedo, love wand, love's picklock, Lucy, lul, lullaby, lunch, lung-disturber, machine, mad mick, maggot, magic wand, main vein, maker, male genital organ, male member, male pudendum, maleness, man steel, man Thomas, manflesh, manhood, manmeat, manroot, man's delight, Marquis of Lorne, marrow bone, marrow bone-and-cleaver, marrow pudding, masculine part, Master John Thursday, master member, master of ceremonies/MC, material part, matrimonial peacemaker, maypole, meat, meat dagger, meat whistle, meatstick, member, member for the cockshire, member virile, membrum virile, mentula, mentule, merrymaker, mickey, middle finger, middle leg, middle stump, milk bone, milkman, millimetre-peter, minus a pinus, Mr. Happy, Mr. Tom, modigger, mole, monster, monster cock, most precious part, mouse, mouse mutton, mow-diewart, muscle, muscle of love,

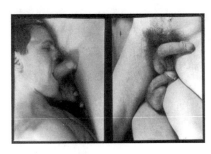

CLARENCE TRIPP, U.S., 1945.
THOMAS WAUGH COLECTION

mutton, mutton dagger, my body's captain, my man Thomas, nag, natural member, nature's scythe, Nebuchadnezzar, necessaries, needle, needle-dick, nervous-cane, nimrod, nippy, nob, nooney, nose, nothin' cock, nudger, nudinnudo, oak tree, Ol' Damocles, old Adam, old blind Bob, Old Faithless, old fellow, old goat-peter, old Hornington, old horny, old man, old root, old slimy, old wary cod, Oliver Twist, one-eyed Bob, one-eyed brother, one-eyed demon, one-eyed milkman, one-eyed monk, one-eyed monster, one-eyed pants mouse, one-eyed trouser snake, one-eyed trouser trout, one-eyed wonder, one-eyed worm, one-eyed zipper snake organ, oscar, our one-eyed brother, P-maker, paper tiger, parts, Pat and Mick, pax-wax, peacemaker, pecker, pecnoster, peculiar member(s), pee-pee, pee-wee, peenie, peezel, peg, pego, pen, penal dick, pencil, pencil dick, pendulum, penie, penis dependens, peppermint stick, Perce, perch, Percy, person, pestle, pet snake, peter, phallus, piccolo, pichicorta, pickira de oro, pickle, picklock, piddler, piece, Piephahn, pike, pikestaff, pile-driver, pilgrim's staff, pillicock, pillock, pimple, pimple-prick, pin, pine, pink cigar, pink oboe, pink torpedo, pinky, pintle, pioneer of nature, pipe, piss pipe, pisser, pissworm, pistol, piston, piston rod, pito, pitonguita, pizell, pizzle, placket racket, plank, plaything, plenipo, plonker, plowshare, plug, plugtail, plum tree, plunger, point, pointer, poker, pole, poll-axe, polyphemus, pondsnipe, pony, pood, poontanger, pooper, poperine pear, popsicle, pork sword, post,

Phallus: Latin; derives from the Greek phallos, *for penis.*
Poontanger: derives from poontang *(intercourse) which in turn is a likely corruption of the French* putain *(whore).*
Rebuilt engine: penis with implant.

potato finger, potent reg-
iment, pots, power, pria-
pus, prick, prickle, pride
and joy, princock, pri-
vates, privy member,
process, prod, prong,
pud, pudding, pulse,
pump, pump-handle,
puny prick, pup(py), pur-
ple-veined tonsil tickler,
puss, putter, putz, pylon,
python, quartermaster,
quickening peg, quim-

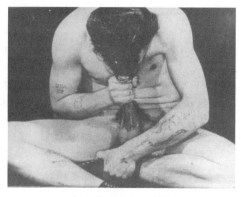

ANON. NETHERLANDS, C. 1960.
THOMAS WAUGH COLLECTION

wedge, quim-stake, rabbit, radish, ralph, ram, rammer, ramrod,
range, rat, raw meat, reamer, rebuilt engine, rector of the female,
red hot poker, red rooster, redcap, rhubarb, rig, rod, rod of love,
Roger, rogering cheat, rogerry, rollin-pin, roly-poly, rooster, root,
Roto-rooter, rotten meat, rubigo, rudder, ruffian, rump-splitter,
Rumplefore-skin, Rupert, Saint Peter, salami, sausage, sceptre,
schlange, schlong, schmekel, schmock, schmuck, schnickel,
Schniedelwutz, Schniepel, schnitzel, schvance, schvont,
Schwanger, schwantz, schween, scope, scorz, scrawny piece,
screwdriver, second head, sensitive plant, sensitive truncheon,
serpent sex, sexing-piece, shaft, shaft of Cupid, shaker, she, shit-
stick, shmendrik, shmok, short arm, short-arm inspection,
short-arm trail, shorty shove-devil, shove-straight, shriveller,
shvants, silent flute, silky appendage, simble, sinbad, Sir John,
Sir Martin Wagstaff, skin flute, skyscraper, Sleeping Beauty,
slug, small, small arm, smell-smock, snake, snake in the grass,
snapper, softy, solicitor general, spar, spear, spigot, spike faggot,
spindle, spit, spitter, split-ass mechanic, split-mutton, split-
rump, sponge, spout, staff, stake, stalk, stallion, star-gazer, steak,
steel rod, stem, stemmer, stern-post, stick, sting, stormy Dick,
strap, stretcher, string, stringbean, strunt, stuff, stump, stupid
dink, sucker, sugar stick, surprise package, swack, sweet meat,
swipe, swiver, swizzle stick, sword, syphilitic prick, tacket, tack-

le, tadger, tail, tail pike, tail pin, tail pipe, tail tree, tail tackle, tally whacker, tantrum tass, tassel, teapot, teeny weeny, tenant-in-tail, tender tumour, tent peg, tentum, that, thing, thingamabob, thingamajig, thingamy, thingummy, thingy, third leg, thistle, Thomas, thorn, thorn in the flesh, throbbing member, throbbing muscle of pure love, thumb of love, tickle-gizzard,

Surprise package: a penis that is bigger than expected.

Thorn in the flesh: a reference to St. Paul's discussion of the torments of sexual temptation.

Portnoy in the novel Portnoy's Complaint *by Phillip Roth spends a lot of time obsessing about his* wang.

Wazoo: a modern American, multi-purpose slang word for rectum, penis, or vagina.

JOHN BARRINGTON, U.K. , c. 1960s.
THOMAS WAUGH COLLECTION

tickle-tail, tickler tink, Timothy, tinkler, tip, tipper, todger, Tom, Tommy, tongue, tonk, tool, tool of pleasure, tootsie roll, torch of Cupid, tosh, tosselberry, tosser-gash, touch trap, tower of lust, toy, trap stick, tree of life, tree of love, trifle trigger, trouble giblets, trouser snake, trout, trumpet, tube, tubesteak, tubesteak of love, tug muscle, tug mutton, tummy, tummy banana, turkey neck, twanger, ugly little dog-dick, Uncle Dick, unit, unruly member, useless, verga, verge, vestry-man, virga, virile member, vomer, wag, wand, wang, wanger, wang bone, wang-tang, wanger, wanker, water spout, water sprout, wazoo, weapon, wedge, wee-man, wee-wee, weenie, well-endowed, well-hung, wet spaghetti, whacker, whammer, whang, whang bone, whanger, what one may call it, whatsit, whatzis, whip, whip whistle, whisky dick, whistle, white meat, white owl, whopper, whore pipe, wick, wiener, wienie, wigga-wagga, willy, wimpy dick, winkle, winky, wire, wong, wood, woofer, worm, wriggling pole, wrinkled dick, wurst, yang, yang fella, yard, yard measure, ying-yang, yosh, yoyo, yum-yum, yutz, zizi, zubb

Penis, Large/Well-Endowed

SEE ALSO PENIS

8/9/10-+, Alfie, ankle spanker, apinniger, ass-spliter, baby's forearm, basket party, beaver cleaver, beer can, big, big basket, Big Ben, Big Bird, big boy, big boy bassoon, big brother, big hunk of meat, big number, BOD, built, bulging, bulging basket, clarkoid, den dick, donkey dick, donkey-rigged, draped, elephant, enormous, four-eleven-forty-four, gallons, giant, gifted, gigantic, good-sized, grand bag,

8/9/10-+: refers to length, in inches
BOD: "Box of death."
Grand bag: a large scrotum.

great big, hand-reared, heavy hung, hefty, honker, horse, horse cock, horse-like, horsemeat, huge, humongous, hung, hung for days, hung like a bull, hung like a horse, hung like a pony, ice-cream cone, jawbreaker, kidney buster, kidney wiper, killer, large, loggerhead, long pole, long pork, lumber, magnum, mammoth, massive, maypole, meat for the butcher, monstrous, monster, Mr. Big, nine-inch knocker, one who straps it to his ankle, oversized, pretty good sized, rammer, rippled yam, shoe shop, sky scraper, sollicker, stacked, swankasa, sword, tall, Texan, Texas longhorn, throat-filling, thumper, tons of meat, VWE, wanger, warlitzer, wazzock, well developed, well-equipped/we, well-furnished, well-hung/wh, well-loaded, whopper, XWE

VWE: very well-endowed.

XWE: extra well-endowed.

Penis, Large (Circumference)
broad, broad-shafter, fat, like a coke can, plump, sausage-thick, thick, thick as a wrist, thickshafted, wide

Penis (Circumcised)
Most medical insurance plans no longer cover circumcision as a medical procedure.
bobbed, chopped, cleaned, clipped, cut, cut out to be a gentle-man, kosher dill, kosher meat, lop cock, low neck, nipped, peeled queen, roundhead, short sleeves, skinned, snapper, sliced, snipped, surgically altered, trimmed, twenty twenty, unkindest cut (the)

Kosher dill: refers to the fact that male circumcision is part of Jewish law.
Snapper: a term for foreskin.

Penis (Small)
agate, baguette, biteful, bugfucker, dinky, bookie's pencil, chick-en wing, dwarf, fingerhoot, hung like a mouse, IBM/itty bitty meat, narrow at the equator, needle dick, pea in a pocket, peed-ie, peepee meat, pee-wee, piccolo, pinky, quatmeat, shetland rabbit, snack, stump, tiddler, tic tac, winkel, winkie/winky

Penis (Uncircumcised)
anteater, blind (be), blind as a boiled turnip (be), blind meat, café curtains, Canadian, cavalier, change purse, chicken neck (small), convertible (vs hard top), end sheath, goatskin, intact, Jewish nightcap, kosher, lace curtains, near-sighted (be), onion skin, opera capes, peapod, religion, ref, skin queen, snaper, tref, turtleneck, uncut (be), unsliced, wink, winkie

Drawing the blinds: pulling back the foreskin.
Docking: when an uncircumcized gay male envelopes the head of his partner's

penis with his foreskin as they masturbate.
Ride a blind piece: to blow an incircumcised man.

Personal Ads (Codes Used for)

24/7 (twenty-four hours/seven days a week, or full time), ALAWP (all letters answered with photo), ASL (age sex location, per Internet chat), B&D (bondage and discipline), BA (bare assed), BBW (big beautiful woman), BF (butt fuck), BLG (bisexual, lesbian, gay), BJ (blow job), BLK (black), BND (boy next door), BO (bottom only), BOYF (boyfriend), BRB (be right back), CA (can accommodate), CBH (can be had), CBT (cock and ball torture), CD (cross dressing), CS (clean shaven), D (divorced), DCV (dress code violator), DD (drug/disease free, DIY (do it yourself :masturbation), DL (down low: appears straight), DM (Doc Martens wearer), DOM (dominant), DP (disabled person), F (female), F2M/FTM (female to male), FF (fist fucking), FOD (friend of Dorothy), FONE FRK (phone freak), FR (French (oral), G (gay), G (Greek (anal), GAGA (gay acting/gay appearing), GAF/GOF (gay Asian/Oriental female) GAM/GOM (gay Asian/Oriental male), GBF (gay black female), GBM (gay black male), GDLK (good-looking), GHM (gay hispanic male), GIB (good in bed), GIRLF (girlfriend), GS (golden showers), GSO (good sense of humour), GSOH (good sense of humour), GWF (gay white female), GWM (gay white male), H (Hispanic), HIV neg/- (HIV negative), HWP (heart-weight proportional), ISO (in search of), J (Jewish), J/O (jack/jerk off), LD (light drinker), LTR (long term relationship), LV (Levis/denim), M (male), M (masochist), M8 (mate), MBA (mutually beneficial arrangement), MSM (men who have sex with men), ND (no drinking or drugs), NDBB (navy denim bell bottoms: uncircumcised), NS (non-smoker), OHAC (own horse and car), ONS (one-night stand), PA (photo appreciated), PA (Prince Albert piercing), PIC (picture), PnP (party and play), POS (positive), PRE-OP (pre-operation), PWA (person with AIDS), S (single), SA/SL (straight acting/looking), SKIN (skinhead), SM (sado-masochism), SRS (sexual reassignment surgery), SS (safe sex), STR8 (straight), SUB (submissive), TP (tatoos/piercings), TT (tit torture), TV (transvestite), TVE (HIV positive), U/C (uncut), VGL (very good looking), W/E (well-endowed), WLTM (would like to meet), WS (water sports: pissing),W (white), VWE (very well endowed)

Sample lesbian codes: F (furriness factor), BL (bi-lez factor), O (out factor), N (nesting desire), SF (silk vs. flannel factor), R (romance factor).

Perverted/Pervert

From the Latin pervertere. The current usage of the word is much less precise. It is used by conservatives to describe someone who is creepy or dangerous. In more radical circles, the word is embraced for its nascent meaning, that is, the possibility to corrupt or be corrupted.

abnormal, bent, berry, creepy, crud, defective, degenerate, depraved, deviant, dirty, dissolute, DOM, dumper, freakish, freaky perv, fuck struck, fucked, geared, gooner, grody, gross, grotesque, heavy breather, into a particular scene, into kink, into sick shit, kinky, marv, odd, off, otway, panty thief, peculiar, perv girl, perv(y), pervie, pervo, prevert, queer, rotten, rough, secko, sick, sick fuck, sid, sinful, smarmy, strange, twisted, twisty, unhealthy, unnatural, viscious, warped, watson, wicked

DOM: "Dirty old man."
Freaky prev: Pacific Northwest term indicating someone whose sexuality or gender is transgressive.
Perv girl: a kinky lesbian.
"Erotic is when you do something sensitive and imaginative with a feather. Kinky is
    when you use the whole chicken." —John Collee

Pornography (Terms Related to)

Pornography is a multi-billion dollar industry and has gained more acceptance in modern culture since the availability of home video. Gay and lesbian porn, however, remains the target of "official" harassment and seizure in Canada and abroad.

adult, adult show, adult theatre, art pamphlet, art photos, beat sheets, beef cakery, beefcake, beefcakery, blow book, blue(y), blue movies, bod-comics, bongo periodical, bongo/rhythm lit, brown shots, boylies, buddy booth, buck book, burlesque, butt book, C sex, C-shot,

Boylies/jazz mags: gay porn magazines.
Buddy booth: a porn stall that allows you to see and/or touch your neighbour.
Beefcakery: gay porn film.
Brown shots: depict the male anus.
Clit lit: 20th-century American term; refers to erotica written by women.

cheesecake, clit lit, clitteratti (female pornstars), cock shots, cockbook, cockfest, compu-smut, computer sex, continental shots, cook books, cum shot, cyber sex, cyber sleaze, cyberporn, dirt, dirty books, eighteen and older, eight pagers, eroducation, face shot, fag mag, fag paper, fag rag, feelthy, film, filth, flick, fluffer, for a

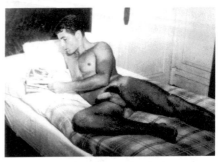

JOHN BARRINGTON, U.K., C. 1960.
THOMAS WAUGH COLLECTION

mature audience only, for adults only, four-letter words, frank, Frankie Vaughan, French photographer, French postcards, fuck film, gayporn, girlie magazine(s), girlie picture(s), girlie show, grumble flicks, hand books,

C-shot: cumshot.
Eight Pagers: refers to porn comix.
Fluffer: a person hired to arouse a male actor prior to filming a sex scene.
French photographer: a 1950s term for a gay photographer.
"The Girlie Show" was the name of Madonna's 1993 tour.

hard porn, hardcore, herotica, hot and heavy, horny porny, jazz mags, jizz biz, leg art, literature gallery, loops, masturbation manuals, mature, money shot, mucky, nasty, naughty, net sex, nuddie/nuddy, nudie, obscenity, open clam shots, page three girl, peepshow, pillow book,

Page three girl: refers to the scantily clad female on page three of certain British tabloids.
Peepshow: from peep or peek, refers to any entertainment involving watching naked women.
Pink shots: depictions of a vagina.
Stroke book or magazine: pornographic print material to which one masturbates.

pin-up boy/girl, pink, pink shots, poopbooth, pop shot, porn, porn shop, porn video, pornbroker, pornie, pornmeister, porno, porny, pornzine, private booth, purple, racy, rank, raunch, ribald, rough, rough stuff, salty, schmaltz, scuzz, sex emporium, sex shop, skin flick, skin house, skin mag, sleaze, smudge, smut, snuff film, softcore, splash shot, split beaver, spread beaver, spread shots, stag mag, stag movie, stag party, steamy, stiffeners, stills, stroke book, stroke house, stroke magazine, suggestive, T&A, Tijuana bible, triple X, video nasty, virtual porn, wank trade, wet shot, wide open beaver, X-rated, XXX

Promiscuous (General)

SEE ALSO AROUSED

Promiscuous has generally been used as a moralistic, judgmental word. Few of these terms suggests affirming attitudes of sexual comfort or freedom. But they're handy if you know someone who's naughty.

after your greens, anatomical, approachable, bestial, can't help yourself, cheap, clinical, coming, crackish, dead easy, degenerate, desperate for it, dissolute, dying for it, easy, easy virtue (of), erogenous, facile, fast, filthy, fond of meat, free-fucking, French, frisky, fruiting, fruity, full flavoured, fun-loving, gagging for it, gay, goatish, has to have it, He-He, helium heels,

He-He: a Vancouver organization founded by performance artist/sex radical Tra la la, who teaches audiences tricks like how to put a condom on a cock without using

your hands. The acronym stands for "Ho's Encoraging the Ho'iness in Everyone."
In the 19th century, being gay meant one who frequented prostitutes. Now the term
refers exclusively to homosexual men and women.
Helium heels: refers to a man whose feet are most often in the air (while being pen-
etrated).
Ho: African-American for whore.

ho, home wrecking, hoee, hot, hot-assed, hot-panted, hot-tailed, humpy, kleenex, knickered, lascivious, lax, lenocinant, lewd, libidinous, lice and fleas, licentious, light, light-heeled, loose, loose in the rump, loose-legged, merry, needs it, nick-nack/nic-nac, obscene, open-fly, pervy, philandering, playsome, radgy, randy, ribald, rig, riggish, rump proud, sexaholic, sexually compulsive, slag, sleazy, sluttish, slutty, spicy, sportful, sportive, sporty, sultry, tentiginous, thick, torrid, trixie, unchaste, uplifting, vestal, wanton, well-bred, whorish, yoyo, X-rated

Wanton: from Middle English wantowen for lewd, without discipline.

Promiscuous Man/Woman (Slut)
SEE ALSO PIMP

The terms for a sexually active or preoccupied male, gay or straight, are much more
forgiving than those used to describe a female libertine, suggesting an enduring
double-standard in sexual attitudes. Gay men have adopted many of the terms for
"loose females" like slut, tramp, and harlot.
adulterer, alley cat, alligator, animal, ass man, avowterer, bad boy, baggage, ballocker, basher, basketeer, bawd, beaver retriever, bed-hopper, bed-presser, belly-buster, big man, bitch (in heat), Bluebeard, bopper, bounder, buck fitch, bull, bum-fiddler, burrduster, cad, campus butcher, carnalite, Casanova, charmer, cheat, cherry-picker, chicken fancier, chicken hawk, chicken queen, chimney sweep, chippy chaser, cock of the walk, cockhound, cocksman, cocksmith, come/cum-freak, con man, Corinthian, cowboy, cradle robber, creep, cur, Delilah, dick, diddler, dirty dog, dirty old man, diver, dog,

Chicken hawk: a gay man who favours young men.
Don Juan: renowned Spanish aristocrat and seducer who carefully documented his many conquests. This expression is still used to suggest a male philanderer, even a gay one.

Don Juan, easy rider, faggot master, faggotmonger, fantail, fast worker, figure-maker, fleece-hunter, flesh-maggot, flesh-monger, floozy, flower-fancier, forbidden fruit eater, foxhunter, franion, fucker, furper, gash hound, gay deceiver, gay dog, gay zombie, getter, gigolo, gin burglar, girler, girltrap, glutton, goat, goer, golddigger, good-for-nothing, groper, grouser, gutter limits, guttersnipe, harlot, headhunter, heaver, heel, helium heels, holer, home-wrecker, horndog, horny bastard, horseman, hot member, hot nuts, hot pants, hound, hussy, Jack Nasty, jezebel, jinker, jumbler, kid stretcher, king of clubs, knocker, lascivious male, lech, leg lifter, leg man, letch, libertine, Lothario, louse, lout, lover, lowlife, lusty guts, make-out artist,

Goat: British term from the 16th century; came to mean lecher likely because goats were "horny" (in both senses) and were also a symbol of sin and the devil.
Lothario: a seducer in the novel The Fair Penitent *by Nicholas Rowe.*

maker, male whore, mammy-jammer, man-killer, masher, meat hound, meat monger, miller, mink, momma-hopper, motherfucker, muck(er), mucky duck, mucky pup, old goat, one who goes for anything that moves, one who loves 'em and leaves 'em, one who sees more ass than a toilet seat, one who takes liberties, operator, Pandora's box, paperboy, parish bull, parish stallion, parlour snake, performer, perv, pervert, philanderer, pimp, pinch-bottom, playa/player, poon hound, predator, prick, prick tease, prigger, profligate, promiscuous male, punker, quail hunter, quim-sticker, rake, ranger, rat,

Rogue: something your grandmother might call a bounder or cad; from the Latin rogare, *to beg (as in beggar, vagabond).*

rattler, ribald gent, rogue, rooster, rounder, rump-splitter, rutter, saloon bar, saloon bar coon, scorekeeper, scum, seducer, sex addict, sexpert, sexual athlete, sexually compulsive male, shag artist, sharp shooter, shifter, skin dog, skirt-chaser, slag, slapper, sleaze, slut bitch/bag, slutbitchwhore, smockster, snake, son of Venus, speed, sperminator, sportsman, squire of the body, stallion, stickman, stinker,  stoat, stringer, stud, swinger, swirver, swordsman, tad, tart, thrumster, tit man, tomcat, tough cat, town bull, town rake, town stallion, troller, tummy-tickler, tramp, twat faker, twigger, user, vixen, wanton, wencher, whisker-splitter, whore, whorella, whorehopper, whoremaster, whoremonger, wild thing, wolf, wood man, yentzer

Stud: early 20th century; suggests an especially virile male and derives from male animals (i.e., horses) used for breeding purposes.
Wolf: early 20th-century American reference to this animal's predatory nature.

Prostitute (Male)

These terms refer to male prostitutes who primarily serve men. Although lesbians are known to consult female sex-trade workers, few modern terms are employed to describe these women. Queer women sex workers are often marginalized by queer and straight society.

30-day boy, ass business (in the), ass peddler, ass-pro, b-boy, baggage boy/box boy, bar hustler, batter, bird taker, bitaine, bit of hard, bitch, body guard, bottle, boulevard boy, box boy, boy, boy fag, boy toy, brown dollars, buff boy, bunny, burn artist, burton, business boy, buttboy, buysexual, calendar kid, call boy, capon, career boy, cash ass, catamite rentboy, champ, charity goods, cheap date,

Baggage boy/box boy: only cock for sale (i.e. will not have anal sex).
Brown dollars: money spent on a gay hustler.
Burn artist: money spent on a crooked hustler.

Charity goods: an unpaid hustler.
Cheap date: a low-priced whore.
Duck: Chinese term for a male prostitute.

chick, chicken, Cinderella fella, cocktail, C.O.D., COD boy, coin collector, commercial boy, cowboy, crack, crack salesman, cyber boy, dial-a-date, dial-a-dolly, dick peddler, dilly boy, dog, dollar-an-inch man, dolly-boy, duck, escort, flat-backer, floater, foot soldier, forty-four, fuck boy, fuck thing, fuck-a-buck, gash, gay for pay, gigolo, girl, goofer, haw your brown, he whore, hide, hole-monger, Hollywood hustler, Hollywood whore, hustler, iron, iron hoof, jag, jumper, KAMP, kife,

Gash: a male prison whore.
Hustler: from the Dutch husselen *meaning to shake or to gain money dishonestly; first used to describe male prostitutes in the 1920s.*
KAMP: "Known as a male prostitute," disputedly the origin of the word camp.
Midnight cowboy: American term from the 1950s. Midnight Cowboy was also a 1969 film starring Jon Voight and Dustin Hoffman about a small-town boy who goes to New York to peddle his wares.

knobber, lease-piece, lobster (marine), lobster pot, masseur, maud, meat, midnight cowboy, Mr. Brown, model, nigh enough, on the bottle, PG rated, paid lover, party boy, pato, pay boy, piece of trade, pink, pink pants, prat boy, prick peddler, pro, pro-baller, punce, punk-kid, purple bob, raggedy android, rent, rented tux, rent boy, renter, road kid, rented tux, Rita, rough trade, salesman, salt-seller, scarlet sister, slut boy, spunk rat, spintry, soldier, sport, sporting goods, sporting girl, stripper, stud for hire, Susan Saliva, telephone hustler, trade, trickmeister, walker, working girl, wrangler, zook

PG rated: gay for pay.
Purple bob: a gay kept man.

Salt-seller: sailor prostitute.
Zook: old gay hustler.

Prostitute (to Prostitute Oneself)

be a pro, be a professional, be in the life, bitchery, buttock ban-
quetting, cover the waterfront, curb/kerb crawling, do escort
work, do massage work, fast life, game (the), go case, go into the
streets, go to Paul's for a wife, hawk your fork, hawk your hook,
hawk your mutton, horizontal life, hustle, Immorality Act,
importuning, in circulation, in the biz, in the business, in the
game, in the trade, life (the), life of infamy, life of shame,

Cover the waterfront: refers to the fact that prostitutes in port towns frequent areas
near the water where eager sailors congregate.
Mrs. Warren's profession: refers to warren as in rabbit colony, rabbits being consid-
ered highly sexed creatures. It was also the name of a 1898 play by George Bernard
Shaw.
The Life was a 1997 Tony Award-winning musical about prostitutes.

live by the trade, lost, love for sale, Mrs. Warren's profession,
nice time, night job, nocturne, old patrol, oldest profession, on
the bash, on the game, on the grind, on the street(s), on the
stroll, on the town, palliardy, peddle your ass, peddle your meat,
peddle your wares, peddle pussy, pound the pavement, pussy
game, putage, quick time, run a brothel, sacking, sell favours,
sell your ass, sell your back, sell your bacon, sell your body, sell
your flesh, sell your desires, sell yourself, show your charms,
sinful commerce, sit on your stuff, social E., soliciting, step,
street of shame, street-tricking, street-walking, strut your stuff,
suburb trade, tail trading, trade (the), tricking, turn out upon the
streets, turn tricks, vice, walk the streets, whoredom, work in a
brothel, work the sidewalk, work the streets

Whoredom: from the Middle English hordom which derived from the Old Norse
hordoms, meaning prostitution.

Prostitute's Client

Most of these terms were invented by male and female sex trade workers and are either demeaning, critical, or contain a warning about specific types of customers. The language suggests solidarity among "working girls."

angel, baby, beef burger, boss trick, champagne trick, bum chaser, bum pusher, client, cold biscuit, cull, curb crawler, customer, daddy, date, fare, freak, freak trick, frequent flyer, friend with money, gonk, jim, jockey, john, live one, meal ticket, meatball, money trick, old man, papa, papa gâteau, patron, payboy, paying customer, piper, punter, rabbit, regular, score, short timer, sugar daddy, tos, thirty-three, trick

Champagne trick: signifies a wealthy customer who can afford bubbly.
John: an American underworld expression for a prostitute's customer, used since the 1940s.
TOS: "Trick off the street."

> *"In each room there is a man who says he is lost. You raise his white ghost from the grave.*
> *Later; his ghost is crumpled in a used tissue, washed away with anti-bacterial soap,*
> *A thumbprint on a hundred dollar bill." —"You are Here (a map) 2003"*
> *by Amber Dawn Upfold*

Pubic Hair (Female)

Many of these male-invented terms are poetic, affectionate, or endearing, in contrast with other terms for female genitalia.

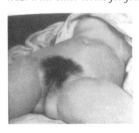

area, assbeard hair, banner, beard, bearskin, beehive, belly bristles, belly thicket, belly whickers, blurtbeard, brakes, Brazilian wax, broom, brush, bugger grips, bush, Bushy Park, carpet, cat skin, clover field, cotton, country, cuffs and collars, cunt down, cunt hair, cunt stubble, down, Downshire, feather, fleece, fluff, flum, forest, forest bush, front door mat, fud, fur, fur pie, fur below, furry, furrybush, furze bush, fuzz, fuzz sandwich, garden, garden hedge, ginge ming, grass, green grove, hair-court, lady's low toupee, hat, lawn, map of Tasmania, leg beard, merkin, moss, mott carpet, muff, mustard and cress, nature's veil, nether eyebrow, nether eyelashes, old Frizzle, parsley, parsley patch, patch, plush, pubes, pumpkin cover, pussy cover, pussy hair,

Brazilian wax: an excruciating, wax-pulling epilation of the vaginal area
Bush: 20th-century term for female pubic hair and genitals in general.
Country: as in cunt-tree.
Pubic, or pubes: from the Latin puber *for adult; i.e., having reached puberty.*

quim bush, quim whiskers, quim wig, ruffles, rug, scrubbing brush, scut, shaving brush, short and curlies, shrubbery, silent beard, snatch thatch, sporran, squirrel, stubble, sweetbriar, tail feathers, thatch, toupee, tuft, twat fuzz, twat rug, velcro strips, whin bush, wool

Pubic Hair (Male)

area, brakes, brillo pad, brush, bush, cotton, dick wheat, Downshire, feathers, Fort Bushy, fud, fur, fuzzies, garden, gorilla salad, grass, lawn, parsley patch, patch, plush, pubes, scrubbing brush, short and curlies, sporran, squirrel, thatch, treasure trail, tuft, wool

Rape (to)

SEE ALSO PENETRATE, FONDLE

A frequent fantasy in queer and straight erotica. From the Latin rapere, *to seize.*
abuse (sexually), assail, assault, attack, bang, break and enter, commit a statutory offense, date-rape, debauch, do, drumstick, dry fuck, force yourself on, force-fuck, gang-bang, gang-rape, gorilla, grab, gross assault, harass, harm sexually, have your way

with, horrorgy, hurt sexually, jam one up, make unwanted advances on, manhandle, molest, perpetrate a sexual crime upon, pillage, plunder, ravage, ravish, ruin, short-arm heist, sodomize, spoil, take, take advantage of, take forcefully, thrash and trash, violate

Rightly so, many references have criminal undertones: break and enter, pillage, plunder, violate.

Rimming

Rimming is a 20th-century American term; refers to the edge of a hole, in this case, used as a verb to describe the practice of licking the anus.

A2M, analingus/anilingus, ass-blowing, biting the brown, black wings, blow some ass, bog snorkeling, brown wings, bum-licking, butt-ramming, canyon yodeling, chokie lips, chutney lingus, cleaning up the kitchen, eating jam, eating poundcake, e. coli pie, feuille de rose, ks (kissing shit), kissing down under,

Anon. U.S., c. 1940.
Thomas Waugh Collection

kissing the star of love, moustache ride, playing the piano, reaming, reamo ream, rim job, rimadonna, rimming, rose leaf, Rosemary, salad queen, sewer-chewing, shoving the tongue, sitting on your face,

A2M: "Ass to mouth."
Feuille de rose: rose petal.
KS: "Kissing shit."
Rimadonna: gay slang for one who enjoys anilingus; a play on the term primadonna.
Salad queen: a man who likes to rim.

smearing the tuna, snarfing, sucking ass, sucking asshole, sugar bowe pie, taking a trip to the moon, telling a French joke, thirty-nine, tip the ivy, tip the velvet, tongue fuck, tongue job, tongue sandwich, tonguing your hole, tossed salad, whitewashing the back (side)

Scrotum

SEE ALSO TESTICLES

bag, ball bag, ball-sack, bozack, clackerboz, cod, hairy saddle-bags, happy sack, knob sack, nadbag, nut sack, pouch, purse, sack, scrote, scrot sack, scrotum parachute, spunk worm, sleep-ing bag, tool bag, twat hammer, winky bag

Scrotum parachute: A studded leather codpiece.
Shakespeare used purse *as a term for scrotum.*

Semen

SEE ALSO EJACULATE (TO), ORGASM
From Latin semen, *for seed.*

albino custard, axle grease, baby custard, baby fat, baby juice, baby paste, ball glaze, beef gravy, beer, blecch, bong spew, boy honey, boycum, boyjuice, bull gravy, bullets, butter, buttermilk, chism, chitty, chuff and chutty, churn, cock porridge, cock snot, cock soup, cock vomit, cockjuice, cocoa butter, come, come-juice, cometosis, comings, cream, cream sauce, crud, cum, Cupid's toothpaste, Cyclops' tears, Cyrus sap, daddy juice, delicious jam, dick butter, dick drink, dickwad, dolly, dream whip, effusion, ejaculate, emok, face cream, farm cum, father stuff, felch, felch mettle, fetch, fizz, fluid, foam,

Cometosis: semen on the breath; a combination of cum and halitosis.
Crud: dried semen on sheets or clothing.
Emok: backward approximation of come.

French dressing, froth, fuck, fuck juice, gentleman's relish, ger-min/german, gism/gissum/gizzum, glop, gloy, glue, goat's milk, gonad glue, goo, gravy, Guinness, guma, herbalz, hocky, home brew, honey, hot fat, hot juice, hot milk, Irish confetti, jack, jam, jazz, jelly, jelly baby, jerk juice, jet stream, jism, jizz, jock juice, joombye, joy juice,

Gism and jism: middle 19th-century; origin unknown, but suggesting spunk, verve.
Goat's milk: bitter tasting semen.
Jelly baby: secretions around the penis or vagina.

juice, junk, lather, letchwater, lewd infusion, liquid, liquid bullets, liquid pearl, liquor sem- inale, load, love, love custard, love juice, love liquid, lumpy piss, mahu poi, man juice, man mustard, man oil, man soup, manhood, manseed, manspunk, maria, marrow, McSpunk, mayonnaise, mecotero, melted butter, mess, mettle, mettle of generation, mez, milk, milt, muckle spat, nad glue, nature, nectar, non-dairy treat, nut, nut butter, oil, oil of man, ointment, oyster, paste, pearl, pearl drop, pearl necklace, pecker

tracks, people paste, plum sauce, pod juice, popu- lation paste, prick juice, protein, pubic hair gel, pudding, reproductive fluid, rice pudding, roe, royal jelly, santorum, scott, scum, seed, semen, semen virile, seminal fluid, sexual discharge, shissom, slime, snake venom, snedge, snowball, snowstorm, soap, soul sauce, spaddel, spaff, span- gle, spendings, sperm,

Mettle: 17th-century English term; from metal suggesting value, stamina.
Pecker tracks: damp or crusty remnants of ejaculate on clothing.
Santorum: technically not semen, but a combination of lube and facal matter that results after anal sex; named by sex columnist Dan Savage for Rick Santorum (R- Pa.), the U.S. senator who in 2003 equated homosexuality with pedophilia and bestiality.
Snowball: mutual exchange by mouth of semen after completing oral sex.
Soul sauce/cocoa butter: the semen of a black man.

Victoria Monk: rhymes with spunk.

spermatic juice, spew, spirit, splooch, splash, splooge, spoo, spooch, spoof, spooge, spoonta, spooze, spratz, spray, spuff, spume, spunk, starch, sticky, sticky seed, stud-lotion, stuff, suds, sugar, tadpole treacle, tail juice, tail water, tallow, tapioca tooth-paste, tread, treasure, Victoria Monk, vitamins, wad, water of life, wazz, whipped cream, white blow, white honey, white love piss, whitewash, whore's milk, yoghurt

Sex Toys and Paraphernalia

SEE ALSO FETISHES, APHRODISIAC, PORNOGRAPHY

Visit your local sex shop if you don't believe that some of these objects are common-ly used in sexual play.

"FLOGGER" WHIP
#WHP01 • $75.00
HANDLE: 6" • METAL LASHES: 22"

Accu-jac, anal violin, ankle cuffs/restraints, aromas, artificial vaginas (Bachelor's friend), auto-suck (electric) vagina, ball toys, ball weights, beaver dams, belts, ben-wa balls, Betty,binding, birch, blindfolds, Blisbos, boots, bullwhips, bulletin boards, butt plugs, cableties, candles, canes, cat o' nine tails, catheters, chains, chastity belts, chocolate, cigars, clamps, clingfilm (i.e., Saran wrap), clothes-pins, cockrings, cockstraps, collars, computers (i.e., on-line), corsets, costumes, Crisco, crops, cuffs, cybersex, denim, dental dams, dildo, douches, duct tape, dungeons, elbow restraints, electric shocks, enema bags, erotic balls, erotica,

Ampallang/apadrayva/dydo/foreskin/frenum/guiche/hafada/lorum: various geni-tal piercings.

Beaver dam: dental dam.

Ben-wa balls: chinese pleasure balls, either loose or stringed, inserted into the vagi-na or anus for stimulation.

Betty: a cowhide whip.

feathers, food, footware, fruit, fur, gaffer's tape, gags, gas masks, genital piercing, glory holes, Godemiche, handcuffs, handkerchiefs, harnesses, high-heeled shoes, hoods, hooks, hot wax, ice cubes, implants, industrial ware, insertive toys, irons, jewellry, jockstraps, KY jelly, lashes, latex wear, leather, leg irons/restraints, love beads, love dolls (inflatable), lube/lubricant, lycra, manacles, mirrors, mud, nasogastric tubes, nipplerings, orogastric tubes, packing/packed,

Dildo: 16th-century English term; may derive from the Italian diletto *meaning delight.*

Godemiche: from a 19th-century French term for dildo.

Horizontal hood: a clitoral piercing.

Other phrases for high-heeled shoes: CFMs (come-fuck-me's), fuck-me pumps.

Peg: to penetrate a man with a dildo.

packing/packed: describes a woman wearing a strap-on dildo or stuffing her pants to give the appearance of a good package. A tactic often used by drag kings.

Suction cups/snake kits: devices used to enlarge nipples.

paddles, paraphallus, penetration toys, penis pumps, phone sex lines, photography, piercings, plastic cock, playrooms, Prince Albert (penis piercing), racks, razors, riding crops, satin sheets, scaffolds, sex toys, sexlines, shackles, slings, specula, spencer paddles, stocks, straightjackets, straps, stretching equipment (i.e., weights), stiletto heels, strap-on dildoes, strings  of pearls, suction cups/snake kits, sutures (infibulation), switches

"Twelve dildoes meant for the support Of aged lechers of the Court . . . Some were composed of shining horns, More precious than the unicorn's. Some were of wax, where ev'ry vein, And smallest fibre were made plain, Some were for tender virgins fit, Some for the large falacious slit, Of a rank lady, tho' so torn, She hardly feels when child is born."
—"Dildoides," Samuel Butler, 17th century

tattoos, telephone, telephone sex, thumb cuffs, tit clamps, tit rings, tourniquets, underwear, uniforms, vacuum pumps, vibrators, video (cameras), waders, wax, whipped cream, whipping posts, whips, wrist cuffs/restraints

Sexually Transmitted Disease(s) (General)

Historically, the naming of STDs has been a farovourite vent for gingoistic name calling.

bad blood, bad disease, bend a pipe on the pisser (to have one), blood disease, blue boar, blue fever, bone ache, boogie, brothel sprouts, bulldog dose, burner, burning (infected), cardboard box, catch a cold, chlamydia, clap, clapp, coals, cock-rot, cold in the dong, communicable disease, crinkums, crud, crunk, Cupid's itch, curse of Venus, delicate disease, dirty barrel, dody boiler, dog (the), dose,

Clap: English term from the 19th century; derived from the French clapper for bordello and clapoir, a genital sore. A generic term for any veneral disease but often specifies gonorrhea.

Double event/full house: suggest a combined infection of gonorrhea and syphllis.

double event, drip, drips (the), dripsy, enviable disease, fire, flame, flap dragon, forget me not, foul disease, foul disorder, four plus, full hand, full house, fungina, garden gout, genital warts, genitourinary disease, give someone a burn, gift giver, gleet, gleets (the), glue, goodyear, goose, gout, green-pee, greens (the), grincums, haircut, Herpes, horse, horse and trap, Irish mutton, itchy-scratchies, jack, ladies' fever, leaking, load, loathsome disease, lobster tails, lues venerea, mala de Franzos, malady of France, marbles, measles, morning drip, nap, nine-day blues, noli me tangere, occupational hazard, old dog (the), old Joe, penis souvenir, pid, pimple, pintle fever, pip (the), piss pins and needles, plague, pox, preventable disease, pussy-pussy, rahl (the), Rhea sisters, rusty rifle, sauce, scabbado, scalder, scrud, secondary, secret disease, sexual disease, siff, sigma phi, snatch monsters, social disease, souvenir, stick, taint (the), token, turnip seeds, venereal, venereal disease/VD, Venus's curse, vice disease, warts, wasp, (the) yellows

PID: pelvic inflammatory disease.
Venereal: from Venus, the goddess of love.

STDs: Gonorrhea

applause, bubonic (i.e., plague), blennorrhea, bube, burner, burn, clap, clapp, clappy, dose of claps, dose (the), drip (the), dripper, dripsy, four-plus, gentleman's complaint/GC, glue, gonny, gonoblenorrhea, gonoblenorrheal infection, gonorita, gonorrheal infection, goodyear, green discharge, hammerhead clap, hat and cap, head cold, little casino, looloo, lulu, morning drop, Neisseria gonorrhea, Neisserian infection, old dose, old Joe, piss green, rash, stick (the), strain

Applause: African-American for the clap.
Four-plus: refers to the quantified microscopic appearance on a slide of the bacteria causing gonorrhea.
Glue: 19th-century English term; from the thick infective secretions caused by gonorrheal infection.
Gonorrhea: a medical term from the Greek gonos, for seed.

STDs: HIV

?VE, A-word (the), AIDS, antibody AB+, ARC, bit by the dog, bug brother(s), bug chaser, gatoraids, gift (the), gift givers, HIV-infected, HIV-negative, HIV-positive, kitty (the)/kitty litter

?VE: unsure of HIV status.
ARC: AIDS-related complex (obsolete).
Bit by the dog: to be HIV-positive.
Bug chaser: someone trying to catch HIV by engaging in unsafe sex.
Innoculation parties: unsafe sex orgies. Their existence may be an urban legend. Also called bareback parties.
PHA: person with HIV or AIDS.
PLWA: person living with AIDS.
Pozcum: HIV-positive semen (also called charged cum).

PWA: person with AIDS.

(AIDS), innoculation parties, it, looking thin, lost a bit of weight, neg, negative, on the cocktail, permanent slimming cure, PHA, PLWA, pos, positive, poz, pozcum, PWA, red ribbon, sero-discordant, sero-negative, sero-positive, sick, slim disease, switch blaids, tested, tested negative, tested positive, TVE

A red ribbon is worn on your coat or shirt as a symbol of personal HIV infection or solidarity with the AIDS political movement.
Silence = Death: anti-AIDS-ignorance slogan (by ACT-UP) circa 1988.
TVE: HIV-positive.

STDs: Hepatitis
active/chronic, bollock rats, hep, hepatitis A, hepatitis B, hepatitis C, jaundice(d), liver disease

STDs: Pubic Lice
ass mites, bosom buddies, bosom chums, bosom friends, chums, cooties, crabs, creepers, critters, crotch critters, crotch crickets, dibs and dabs, dick scorpions, gentleman's companion, lap bugs, lice, light troops, love bugs, nits, pant rabbits, pubic visitors, Sandy McNabs, seam squirrels, shattis, taxi

Crabs: from the crab-like microscopic appearance of pubic lice.

STDs: Syphilis
Syphilis, a once fatal sexually transmitted disease which led to madness and paralysis, was named after the protagonist of a 16th-century Italian poem by Fracastoro.
band in the box, bang and biff, big casino, blood disease, boogey/boogie, chancre, clap, coachman on the box, English disease, French crown, French disease, French goods, French gout, French pox, Jack-in-the-box, malady of France, measles, mesosyphilis, Morbus Gallicus, Morbus Hispanics, Morbus

Indicus, Morbus Neopolitanus, Neapolitan, Neapolitan bone ache, Neapolitan consolation, Neapolitan disease, Neapolitan favour, Nervo and Knox, Phyllis, pox, primary syphilis, ral/rahl (the), Reverend Knox, siff, sigma phi, siph, six-oh-six, social disease, Spanish gout, Spanish needle, Spanish pox, specific ulcer, syph, sypho, tertiary syphilis, Venus's curse

Band in the box, coachman on the box, jack-in-the-box and others rhyme with pox.
Chancre: the telltale ulcer on the genitals signifying early infection with syphilis.
Neapolitan disease: a 17th-century term which alludes to the notion that Naples was the origin of syphilis.
Spanish pox: popular in the 19th century, suggesting the frequent connection of jingoistic and sexual fears.

Sexually Transmitted Disease (to Catch)
catch a cold, catch something, contract an STD, cop a dose, get burned, get dosed up, get infected, get sick, get VD, get/have a leaky faucet, give someone a burn, have a discharge, have the nine-day blues, infected (be), jacked up (be), one of the knights (be), pick up a nail, piss white, piss broken glass, piss green, piss pins and needles, piss pure cream, piss yellow, ride the silver steed, strain, take the bayonet course

Give someone a burn: to infect with an STD.
Be jacked up: a modern Australian expression which may derive from jack-in-the-box.

Sexy: SEE ATTRACTIVE FEMALE, HANDSOME MALE

Sissy: SEE EFFEMINATE, FEMME

Slut: SEE PROMISCUOUS MAN, PROMISCUOUS (GENERAL)

Sodomite (Including Top/Bottom)
SEE ALSO GAY (HOMOSEXUAL) MALE

Many of these terms are derogatory. Coined by heterosexual men, most reflect either discomfort or disgust with the notion of anal intercourse between men. Modern slang differentiates between the top giver and the bottom receiver in anal intercourse.

"All roads lead to Sodom." —Evelyn Waugh

active, active sodomist, anal intruder, anal rampooner, anal scientist, angel, angelina, archangel, ass-bandit, ass-bead, ass-farmer, ass-fucker, ass-goblin, ass-jabber, ass-king, ass-man, ass-master, ass-pirate, ass-pro, ass-shark, ass-thrasher, asshole liaisons officer, asshole buddy, ass-tronaut, backdoor buddy, backdoor milkman, backgammon player, backgammoner, back-seat driver, bird-taker, birdie, botter, bottom, bottom man, bottom surgeon, bottomite, brown admiral, brown hatter, brownie king, brownie queen, bucket boy, bud sallogh, bufu, bug, bug-gah, bugger, bum bandit,

Buggery: an English term used since the 16th century; derived chauvinistically from the Latin bulgaris or the Bulgars, who allegedly practiced anal intercourse.

bum plumber, bumboy, bum-fucker, bun-duster, bun-spreader, bunghole bandit, bunker, burglar, butt slut, buttfuck buddy, catcher, cheeks-spreader, chocolate starfish collector, chutney ferret, cinaedus, colon-bowler, cornholer, corvette, Daddy, diddler, eye doctor, fart-catcher, father-fucker, felcher, fudge-packer, gentleman of the back door, gooser, gut-buster, gut-butcher, gut-fucker, gut-reamer, gut-scraper, gut-stretcher, gut-stuffer, Hershey Bar boy, hot buns, insertee, insertor, inspector of man-holes, jesuit, jockey, joey, ky queen, lick box, lucky pierre, mason, member of the brown family, passive, pederast, pitcher, Prussian, puff, reamer, ring-snatcher, rump-ranger, sheep-herder, shirt-lifter, shit-hunter, shit-stirrer, sod, sodomist, stern-chaser, stuffer, sweet cheeks, sweetcakes, top, trick, turd bandit, turk, uncle, uphill gardener, uranist, usher, wolf

Sodomite (Bottom)

Can be used as a noun or a verb.

b-boy, baggage boy, bitch, bottee, boy hole, bronc/bronk, brownie, brownie queen, buey, bum boy, bum bandit, butterfly, caboose, catcher, fuck boy, gunsel, greek, half a man, mampala/mampala-man, mancunt, man hole, Martha, mattress muncher, passive, peg boy, pick up the soap, pogue, quean, receiver, sarong, todge, wears his keys on the left

Half a man: 1970s African-American term for a passive gay male.

Sodomite (Top)

Can be used as a noun or a verb.

active, anal jabber, Arthur, bang artist, bandit, biscuit, BK, body guard, boffer, booty bandit, boretto man, botter, brown artist, brown batter, brownie king, bucket, buey, bugger, bummer, bun bandit, banger, burger, butch number, caboose, cornholer, deadeye dick, eye doctor, fudge packer, gandler, giver, gonif, Greek active, gut stretcher, hemorrhoid hitman, hip hitter, hoola raider, humper, indorser, jobby jonster, jocker, keester bandit, king, pitbull top, pitcher, porker, pratt man, punker, rear specialist, rider, ring snatcher, top man, truck driver, turd packer, Turk, wears his keys on the right

Versatile: likes to be a top and a bottom. Many bottoms claim they are versatile.

Sodomize (to)

A, a-buck, analize, ask for the ring, ass-fuck, bend some ham, bend someone over, boop, bottom, brown (to), buckswing, bumfuck, bunghole, burgle, bury your bone in the backyard, bury your ring, butcher knife, butt-fuck, buttplug, commit pederasty, cop your rosebud, cornhole, daisy chain, dig a ditch, dive into the sky, dot the "I," duke, fish for brown trout, flip over, foop, fuck, get a paint job, get hunk, get some brown sugar, go Hollywood, go up the old dirt road, grease, grease and lease, Greek, haul someyour ashes, have a bit of Navy cake, hose, keister-stab, ingle, lay the leg, lift your shirt, manhole, pack peanut butter, paint, pancake, pipe, plank, play leapfrog, plow, plug, pogue, poke, polk, pork, pound your ass, pound your cheeks, pound your butt, power-fuck, punk, push shit uphill, rectify, ride your deck, shit fuck, shoot in your tail, shoot your star, snag, sod, sodomize, spread your ass, spread your butt, spread your cheeks, stir fudge, stir shit, take it up the ass, take the Hershey highway, throw a buttonhole on, tom finch, tom fuck, top, tunnel, turn over

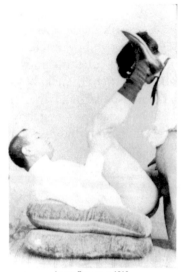

ANON. FRANCE, C. 1910.
THOMAS WAUGH COLLECTION

Sodomy

Sodomy *was historically a generic term for "unnatural sexual practice" including both oral and anal sex.*

abort, a-buck, amor, anal acts, anal dance, anal delight, anal intercourse, anal job, anal lovemaking, anal tobogganning, ass fucking, ass games, back jump, backdoor boogie, back-door work, back scuttle,

Abort: to defecate after anal sex.
Amor: Roma *spelled backwards. Refers to the supposed prediliction of ancient Romans to engage in anal sex.*
Bareback: anal intercourse without a condom.
Broom in a cave: performing anal sex on a partner who is a tad loose from much experience.
The cookies: U.S. hip-hop term for anal sex.

backshot, baiting the hook, baking potatoes, balling, banging fudge, bareback/BB, behind the behind, bending some ham, bit of brown, bit of bum, bit of tail, blessing (a), boody, Bosco boulevard, bottle, bottom's up, broom in a cave, brown, browning, buggery,bung holing, butt-balling, butt-banging, butt-fucking, butthole surfing, buttplay, cookies (the), celebrity pumping, chocolate cha-cha, coitus in ano, coitus per anum, cornholing, daub of your brush, digging a ditch, dinner mashing, dipping in your fudge pot, dog in the bathtub, double entry drop the soap, dry date fall harve (the), fishing for brown trout, flip and dick, fluffing the duff, going up your ass, going up your chute, going up the mustard road, Greek, Greek culture, Greek love, Greek way, higher Malthusianism,

Double entry: penetration by two penises.
Flip and dick: gay rape.
Harva (the full): Polari for anal intercourse.
Malthusianism: a notion of population control in the 19th century described by
Malthus; hence a reference to keeping the population down through non-procreative
sex, i.e., anal intercourse.
Raw dog: anal sex without a condom.

hoop, Irish, kiester stab, kneeling at your altar, mustache, navy style, packing fudge, peanut butter, pig-sticking, pile-driving, playing dump truck, popping it in your toaster, prat for (to), predication, ram job, ramming, raw dog, riding your deck, saddling it up, sixty-six, shit fuck, sitting on it, sodomizing, sunnyside up, taking it up the ass, trip to the moon, unmentionable vice, unnatural acts, unnatural connection, unnatural debauchery, unnatural offense, unnatural sexual intercourse, unnatural vice, up the butt

Sperm: SEE SEMEN

Stripper/Stripshow

booth dance, bottomless, boy show, boy-girl show, bubble dancer, bump and grind, bumper, burlesque, burlesque artist, chomp, contact (allowed), cooch, couch dance, couple act, ecdysiast, European-style peeling, exotic, exotic dancer, exotic dancing, fan dancer, feature dancer, flasher, floor show, Gaiety (the), girl show, girlesque, girlie show, grinder, hardcore show, hootchy-kootchy, lapdance(r), lingerie model, live sex model, live sex show, live show, male dancer, male stripper, no contact (allowed), peeler, personal show, pole dancer, private dance,

The Gaiety: a famous New York City gay strip joint.
Girlesque: combines girl and burlesque.
Petting zoo: a strip joint where touching is allowed.
PSP: "pornstar peeler."
Some strip clubs for straight men now have private rooms where women dance for women.

petting zoo, private dancer, PSP, pussy dance, pussy dancing, ripper, sex model, shake and shimmy, shower act, shimmy, slinger teaser, stag show, stripathon, striptease artist, table dancing, take in, teabagging, tit(ty) bar, topless, topless dancer, toss back, tosser, towel dance, uncover boy, uncover girl, weaver

Teabagging: referenced in the John Waters film Pecker, *describes the dipping action of a male stripper who bobs his testicles on his customer's head.*

Sweetheart (Male and Female)
SEE ALSO GIRLFRIEND, BOYFRIEND

These terms, shared by gay and straight people, are among the most delightful in the book. They are affectionate, endearing, and relational.

babe, baby, baby doll, babycakes, bint, bird, biton, blue serge, boobie, boy, boyfriend, bubbie, bunny, chicken pie, cupcake, cutie, darling, dear heart, dearie, doll, dreamboat, duck(y), dumpling, flame, girl, girlfriend, heartthrob, hon(ey), honey child, honey man, honeybunch, honeybunny, honeycakes, johnny, lambchop, lambkins, main man, main squeeze, my gal, number one, O and O, old flame, only one, patootie, pet, pumpkin, snookums, snuggles, sugar, sugar plum, sunshine, sweet(s), sweet pea, sweetie pie, tootsie

Tootsie, starring Dustin Hoffman, was a hit film in 1983.
O and O: "One and only."

Testicles

See also Scrotum

accoutrements, acres, allsbay, almonds, apples, Arabian goggles, baby makers, ballocks, balls, bangers, bannocks, basket, baubles, beans, Beecham's pills, berries, birds' eggs, bobbles, bogga, bogs, bollocks, boobles, booboos, boolies, boys, bullets, bumballs, buttons, callibisters, cannonballs, Charlies, charms, chestnuts, Chicken McNuggets, chumblies, churns, clangers, clappers, clock weights, cluster, cobbler's stalls, cobblers, cobbs, cobs, cods, coconuts, cods, coffee stalls, cojones, come/cum factories,

Allsbay: pig Latin for balls.
Arabian goggles: the act of resting your testes on a partner's eyes.
Cojones: from the Spanish slang for testes, also as with balls, suggest a link between sexual and social courage.

crown jewels, crystals, cubes, cullion(s), culls, damsons, danglers, diamonds, ding-dangs, ding-dongs, do-dads, do-hickeys, dobblers, dusters, eggs, eggs in the basket, essentials, family jewels, family treasures, flowers, flowers and frolics, Frick and Frack, fun and frolics, future, ghands, gingambobs, glands, goolies, gonads, gooly, gooseberries, grand bag, hairy saddle-bags, happysacks, higgumbobs, jatz crackers, jewels, jiggum-bobs, jingleberries, John Waynes, jungleberries, kanakah, kanakas, kelks, knackers, knockers, ladies' jewels, lam pah, les accessoires, love apples, love nuts, low-hangers, magazines, male mules, man-balls, marbles, marshmallows, monster-balls, monsters, mountain oysters, nackers, nadgers, nads, nags, nards, necessaries,

Fun and frolics: rhymes with bollocks.
Nads: from gonads, a medical term for testes and ovaries.
Orchids: from the Greek orchis for testicle.
Quongs: Polari for testes.

Niagara Falls, nicknacks, nogs, nuds, nuggets, nutmegs, nuts, orbs, orchestra stalls, orchestras, orchids, orchs, orks, orna-ments, oysters, painter's eyes, peanuts, pebbles, pig's knockers, pills, plums, pods, potatoes, pouch, pounders, prunes, quongs, raisin bag, rocks, rollies, rollocks, royal jewels, sack o' nuts, sad-dle bags, scalloped potatoes, scrotum, seals, seeds, sex glands, slabs, slashers, splashers, spunk factories, spunk holders, squir-rel food, stones, swingers, tallywags, tarriwags, taters, testes, tes-ticules, testiculus, testimonials, thingamajigs, thingumbobs, thingummies, Tommy Rollocks, trinklets, twiddle-diddles, twins (the), velvet orbs, vitals, wank tanks, wedding kit, wedding tack-le, whirligigs, winky bag, yarbles, yongles

Threesome: SEE MENAGE À TROIS

Top/Bottom: SEE SODOMY, FETISHES

Transsexual/Transgendered

The language to describe gender variance is changing rapidly. Many of these terms are so new or localized they require explanation. Some of them are derogatory and suggest outdated attitudes to sex-reassignment. Refer to the works of trans activists

like Kate Bornstein if you aren't sure about usage.
bender, berdache, binder, bio-boy, born/genetic female, boy-girl, chick with a dick, chickboy, Copenhagen capon, Danish pastry, dude, FTM, F2M, gender bender, gender disphoric, gender reassigned, gender fluid, gender fuck(er), genderqueer,

Berdache: an alternate gender role in many traditional Native Indian societies. Male-born, but androgynous, they dressed in a mixture of men's and women's clothing and did women's work. They had a special role in their community, performing marriage counselling, taking care of children and often having sex with men.
Binder: anything from a tensor bandage to corset that a trannie boy uses to bind his breasts down.
Bio boy: Biologically male.
Born/genetic female: term for a born woman.
Danish pastry/one who is going to Denmark: Denmark was one of the first countries in the world to offer sex-change operations.
Dude: used to address anyone who prefers masculine pronouns.
FTM: female-to-male transsexual; MTF: male-to-female transsexual.
Gender fuck: to conciously challenge traditional views regarding gender.

he-she, hegal, hem, HIR, ir, katoy, ladyboy, MTF, MTM, manshee, new woman, non-op, on hormones, one who is going to Denmark, per, post-op, pre-op, pre-op trannie, queerqueer, remould, sex-reassigned, shaver, s/he/sie, she-he, she-male, shim, stealth mode, SRS, swan, TG, T Girl, trannie, trannie boy, trans man, transectional, transensual, transfag, transie, transit van, transitioning, transparency, tryke, ts, turnabout, 24-hour girl, W2M, X men,

MTM: a FTM who never acknowledged female gender.
New woman: MTF post-op transsexual woman.
Re-mold: Polari for sex change.
Shaver: a MTF who shaves off her body hair.
SRS: sex-reassignment surgery.
Stealth mode: when a transgendered person lives full-time in their preferred gender.

TG: transgendered.
Transfag: a gay FTM.
Transitioning: in the process of changing genders.
Tryke: a lesbian MTF.
24-hour girl: living in girl gender full-time.
X men: refers to FTMs because, unlike their male-born counterparts, they possess two X chromosomes.

Transvestite

A man or woman who dresses in clothing of the "opposite sex," for performance or fetish reasons.

bender, berdache, bone smuggler, broad boy, chick with a dick, colour TV, cross-dresser, cybertranny, drag baton, drag king, drag queen, drag show performer,

Cross-dresser is often used for heterosexual men who enjoy wearing women's clothes.
Cybertranny: someone who pretends to be the opposite sex online.
Drag king: a woman who dresses as a man for performance.
Drag queen: refers specifically to a gay male who dresses as a woman for show.
Draggette: a young drag queen.
En drab: dressed per boring traditional gender role.
En femme: dressed as a glam woman.
FTV: a female transvestite.

PHOTO: MICHAEL V. SMITH

Eonist, female impersonator, fimp, FTV, gender bender, genetic girl, glamazon, handbag rustler, hir, house mother, in drag, in full-drag, in half-drag, Miss Thang/Thing, mister sister, one who enjoys being a girl, one who gets all dolled up, one who loves lingerie, panty doll, passing woman (female), phallus girl, shim, sie, skag drag, T-fuck, trannie/tranny, transie, TV

Skag drag: a drag queen whose maleness shines through.
T-fuck: sex with a tranny.

Unattractive Man/Woman

SEE ALSO ATTRACTIVE MALE AND ATTRACTIVE FEMALE

Cruising and dishing cruel remarks is a gay pastime only slightly more popular than cruising for anonymous sex in dark places.

bad news, bag, bag/boy, bag-lady, BATS, B-flat omee, boiler, boot, broke, buffarilla, bunter, butt-ugly, cacky, chammy, charity case, chew your arm off, curb, dog, double bagger, douchebag, fugly (fucking ugly), future, geek, hag, hair-don't/scare-do, hilda, ill piece, India, moose, NTBH, ug, pity fuck, PT/profile trap, pug, skag, skank, skeeza, tabby, TBATF, totaled, uggly

Hair-don't/scare-do: an unattractive hairstyle.
BATS: "Better (looking) across the street."
B-flat omee: Polari for a fat bloke.
Chew your arm off: a one-night stand so ugly that you'd rather chew your arm off than waken him when you flee the room.
Double bagger: for the old joke: someone so ugly he wears two bags over his head, in case the first one breaks.
NTBH: "Not to be had."
PT/profile trap: a man who is good-looking sideways but a fright head-on.
TBATF: "Too bad about the face."
> *"My dear, you used to be quite a dish, now you're quite a tureen."*
> *—Somerset Maugham to a lover*

Underwear (General)

Although revealing ads for underwear abound in most contemporary magazines, these articles of clothing were called unmentionables earlier in this century.

Alan Whickers, aesthetically impaired, ass curtains, ass rug, articles, bag, bathers' bloomers, bathing costume, belongings, big eighths, bikinis, bills, bloomers, bodystocking, booger, breech, breeches, breeks, britches, brogues, bull ants, bull's aunts, bum bags, bum curtain, butt floss, buttsack, calf clingers, Calvins, continuations, cossie, costume, cotton hammock, council houses, cozzie, denims, don't name 'ems, drumstick cases, dung hampers, draws, dungarees, east and west, eelskins, farting crackers, fleas and ants, Frenchies, fright (a), frillies,

Bloomers: probably named after Amanda Bloomer, an American advocate of women's rights in the 1800s.
Butt floss: a modern-day American term that originated in California, referring to a string (thong) bikini which rides between the buttocks.
Cossie/cozzie/costume: Australian swim trunks.
Frenchies: French lace underwear.

galligaskins, gallyslopes, gam cases, gaskins, ham cases, hams, holy falls, indescribables, indispensables, inexplicables, inexpressibles, innominables, insects and ants, iron underpants, irrepressibles, jeans, jolly rowsers, kick, kicks, kicksies, kicksters, knickerbockers, knickers, lace panties, lacies, leg bags, leg covers, Levi's, limb shrouders, lingerie, long ones, Mary Walkers, mustn't mention 'ems, nether-set, nether garments, never mention 'ems, nut-chokers, pair of drums, pantaloons, panties, pants, pantyhose, passion killer, plus-fours, rammies, rank and riches, Reg Grundies, Reginalds, reswort, rice bags, rips, ripsey rousers, round me houses, round mes, round the houses, rounds, sacks, scanties, scanty pants, scanty trousers, scarella, scratches, shreddies, sin hiders, sit down upons, sit upons, skilts,

Iron underpants: control-briefs for women.
Unlike North America, pants in the U.K. usually refers to underpants, whereas trousers represents long pants.
Reg Grundies: rhymes with undies.
Shreddies: torn underwear.
Swimmers and togs: swimsuits.
VPL : "Visible panty line."

slip, song and dance, stove pipes, striders, strides, strossers, swimmers, tank top, teddy, thingumabobs, thunderbags, tights, togs, trolly wags, trolly wogs, trolleys, trou, trouserloons, trousies, trucks, uncles and aunts, undergarments, underthings, ug, ug-ly, unhintables, unmentionables, unspeakables, unthinkables, unutterables, unwhisperables, VPL, winter woolies, woolies, Y-fronts

Underwear (Male)

ball-slinger, ballsack, banana hammock, bikini briefs, bitches, bottoms, boxers, buds, Calvins, cockrag, eelskins, grape smuggler, hector protector, jock, jockstrap, Jockeys,

Calvins: refer to Calvin Klein underwear, a favorite of gay men.
Hector protector: jockstrap.
Jockeys: an American brand name of men's briefs, now becoming generic in references to men's underwear.
Speedos: refers to brand-name swimsuit, usually skimpy.

kecks, knickerbockers, loincloth, longjohns, lunchbox, pants, ripsey rousers, shorts, skivvies, snood-hood, snuggies, snugs, Speedo(s), thong, undies, willie-warmer, Y-fronts

Urethra

SEE ALSO GENITALIA
From the Greek ourethra, *and* ouron *meaning urine.*
hole, one-eye, pee-pee, pee-hole, pipi, piss-slit, pisser, urinator

Urinate

SEE ALSO FETISHES, UROPHILIA
answer nature's call, answer the call of nature, bleed the liver, bog, bubble and squeak, burn the grass, check your ski rack, damage the Doulton, dicky diddle, diddle, do a rural, do wee, drain, drain your rad, drain your radiator, drain your snake, drain your crankcase, drain your dragon, drain your lizard, drain your main vein, drain the snake, drain the suds, draw off, ease yourself, empty your bladder, evacuate your bladder, excuse yourself from the table, extract your Michael, extract your urine, find a haven of rest, flesh fanny at the Fowlers, flog your lizard, freshen up, Geoff, get rid of your bladder matter, go potty, go for a snake's (hiss), go look at the crops, go to Egypt, go to the bathroom, go to the loo, have a golden shower, have a gypsy's, have a

jimmy, have a leak, have a piss, have a run-out, have a slash, have a splash, have an accident, heed nature's call, hey-diddle-diddle, hi diddle diddle, hit-and-miss, Jerry Riddle, jim, Jimmy Riddle, Johnny Bliss, kangaroo the dunny seat, kill a snake, kill a tree, kill the grass, lag, leak, let flow, let fly, let 'er rip, let whiz, make, make a branch, make a coke stop, make a phone call, make a piss stop, make a pit stop, make a puddle, make pee-pee, make water, make wee-wee, micturate, nature stop,

Jerry Riddle/Jimmy Riddle: rhyme with piddle.
Micturate: a current medical term from the Latin mictus/mingere, *"to urinate."*
Shake the lettuce: a rare reference to female urination.

number one, pass urine, pass water, pay a visit, pee, pee your pants, pee-break, pee-wee, perform the work of nature, pick a daisy/flower, piddle, piss, pit stop, plant a sweet pea, pluck a rose, point percy at the porcelain, post a letter, powder your nose, preeze, pump, rack off, relieve yourself,  retire, run off, say, scatter, see a dog about a man, see a star about a twinkle, see Johnny, shake a sock, shake hands with an old friend, shake hands with the unemployed, shake hands with the wife's best friend, shake the dew off your lily, shake the lettuce, shed a tear, slack, slash, sling your drizzle, snake's hiss, spend a

 penny, splash, splash your boots, spray, spray the bowl, spray the porcelain, spring a leak, squat, squeeze your lemon, squirt, stimble, strain your green, strain your pota-toes, strain your spuds, strain your taters, syphon off, syphon your python, take

(your) dog for a walk, take a leak, take a pee, take a piss, take a slash, take a walk, tap a keg, tap a kidney, tiddle, tinkle, toy-toy, train Terrence at the terracotta, twinkle, visit Miss Murphy, visit the sand box, void, wash, wash your hands, wash up, water a hedge, water the pony, water the dragon, water the horses, water the roses, wazz, wee, wee-pee, wee-wee, wet, whiz, widdle, wring your your rattlesnake, yellow showers, you and me

Urine
SEE ALSO URINATE, UROPHILIA

flow, lemon juice, lemonade, little jobs, number one(s), pee, pee-pee, piddle, piss, Robert E., snake's hiss, stream, tea, water, wee-wee, whiz/wizz, widdle

Snake's hiss: modern-day Australian term; rhymes with piss.

Urophilia
SEE ALSO URINATE (TO)

German, golden showers/GS, likes it wet, piss scene(s) (into), piss-lover, stream queen, tinkle queen, tinker-belle, urolognia, water sports/WS, yellow hankie, yellow queen, yellow stream queer

Stream queen/tinkle queen/yellow queen: a gay man who enjoys water sports.
Yellow hankie: wearing a yellow handkerchief is a code for enjoyment of water sports.

Vagina
SEE ALSO GENITALIA (FEMALE), LABIA, CLITORIS

Many of these once derogatory terms have been reappropriated or modified by lesbians. Others can be found in use unabashedly in hard-core lesbian porn.

ace, alley, alpha and omega, altar of love, anchory thatch, apple, artichoke, article, Aunt Annie, axe wound, bacon sandwich, bag,

bag of tricks, bank, barge, bazoo, bearded leisure centre, beaver, beaver cake, beefbox, beehive, berk (Berkshire hunt), best, best part, bit, bite, black box, black hole, black joke, black ring, blind alley, blind entrance, blind eye, blurt, boat, bob and hit, booty, Boris, bottomless pit, break like a shotgun, box, bull's eye, bumshop, bun, butcher's window, buttonhole, cake, camel toes, can, canyon, carnal trap, case, cat, cat with its throat cut, cave, cellar, central cut, cha-cha, Charlie, chasm, chimney, chopped liver, chuff, circle, clabby, cladge, cleft, clodge, cock, coffee shop, coinslot, cono, cooch, cookie, coot, cooter, cooze, coozle, crack, cranny, crease,

Artichoke: a poetic metaphor for vagina, referring to that plant's leaves, and the sensuous pleasure of peeling and eating the flesh beneath them.
Cha-cha: hip hop term for vagina.
Cooch: 20th-century American term; derived from hootchy-kootchy, *a playful erotic dance.*
Cunt: highly vulgar term, still in use, from the Middle English count(e), *which derived from the Germanic kunton.*

crevice, critter, cookie jar, cunnicle, cunny, cunt, cylinder, damp, dark meat, dead end street, den, dicky do, diddle, Diddly pout, ditch, divine scar, dormouse, down there, drain, everlasting wound, fadge, fan, fanny, fanoir, fig, finger pie, fireplace, flange, flesh wallet, fleshy part, fluff, fly-trap, fork, fornicator's hall, front bum, front door, front garden, fuckhole, fud, fur, fur chalice, furburger, furrow, furry hoop, furry let- 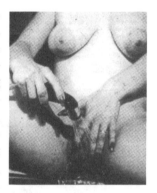 terbox, furry mongoose, futy, futz, fuzzburger, fuzzy cup, G (goodies), G-spot, gap, gape, garden, garden of Eden,

Eastern (Indian/Tibetan) terms for the vagina are often gentle and poetic:
enchanted garden, full moon, great jewel, lotus blossom, moist cave, pearl,

ripe peach, valley of joy.
Gasp and grunt/grumble and grunt/sharp and blunt: rhyme with cunt.

gash, gasp and grunt, gee, gib teenuck, ginch,
gloryhole, golden doughnut, greasebox, gristle
mutt, groceries, groin, grotto, growl(er), grumble
and grunt, grunt, gulf, gully, gullyhole, gutter,
gym/gymnasium, hair pie, hairy pipi, hairy
wheel, hairy whizzer, hanging basket, harbour of
hope, hatch, heaven, hee, hefty clefty, hell, ho
cake, hole, hole of holes, Holiday Inn, home
sweet home, honey altar, honeypot, hoop, horse collar, hot meat,
hot pussy, hotel, house under the hill, Irish fortune, it, Jack and
Danny, jam, jam donut, jambag, jampot, janey, jellybag, jellybox,
jellyroll, Jenny, jewel, jing-jang, Joe Hunt, joxy, joy trail, kebab
wallet, kennel, kettle, kipper trench, kitchen, kitty, kittycat,
knish, knocker pie, ladder, ling, little Mary, little sister, lock,
lodge, lover's lane, lucky bag, lunch box, Maggie's pie, magpie's
nest, map of Tazzy/Tasmania, masterpiece, maw, meat, Mickey
Mouse, middle-cut, minge, mink,

House under the hill: refers to the abode found below the hill, or mons pubis.
Mickey Mouse: the Disney Corporation is likely displeased with this 20th-century
American usage for vagina.

money box, monkey, moot, mouse, mouse's ear, muffin, mutton,
nappy dugout, nasty, nasty gash, nest, nether end, nether mouth,
niche, nodder, nooker, nooky, notch, nursery, old thing, Olympic
pool, open C, open charms, oracle, orgasm chasm, orifice, oven,
P, P-maker, padlock, pancake, papaya, passage, passion pit, pee
Open C: historically, vulgar slang words were often referred to by their first letters
only—in this case, C for cunt.
PEEP: "Perfectly elegant eating pussy."

hole, PEEP, penocha, pie, pink, pink care, pink eye, pink palace
in the Black Forest, pipe, pit, pit hole, pit mouth, pit of darkness,

placket, pocket, poes, poke hole, pole hole, pond, poodong, poon, poontang, pooz, poozle, portal of Venus, pouter, power "U," premises, prime cut, puddin, pulpit, pulse, punani, purse, puss, pussy, pussycat, quic, quiff, quim, quim nuts, quiver, rag box, rattlesnake, receiving set, red lane, ring, rocket socket, rose, rosebud, rubyfruit,

Puss: originally an affectionate English term for a woman, but pussy came to have a more sexual (genital) meaning by the mid-17th century.
Quiff: may be derived from the Italian cuffia *(coif) referring first to hair, then possibly pubic hair.*
Rubyfruit Jungle: a famous lesbian novel by Rita Mae Brown.
See You Next Tuesday: first letters suggest spelling of cunt.

rufus, rump, safe, salt cellar, salmon sandwich, scat, second hole from the back of the neck, see you next Tuesday, sex, sharp and blunt, skin chimney, slice of life, slit, slot, sluice, smoo, snag, snapper, snapping puss, snapping turtle, snatch, snippet, south pole, southerner, spadger, split, split apricot, split beaver, squack, stank, stench, stink, stinkpot, sugar basin, tail, target, Texas snapping turtle, that there, till, toolbox, toot toot, treasury, trench, trim, trout, tube, tuna, twat, twim, twot, vacuum, vag, velvet underground, Venus' glove, vertical smile, vicious circle, Virginia, wallet, where the monkey sleeps, where uncle doodle goes, white meat, woo-woo, wound, Y (the), yoni, you know where, yum yum

Twat: vulgar English term from the 17th century, origin unknown.
Yoni: a sacred sanskrit term suggesting the great womb of creation.

Vaginal Secretions

SEE ALSO AROUSED

crust, cunt juice, discharge, drip, female come, female ejaculation, female spendings, froth, getting ready, girl cum, goose grease, gravy, gunk, lather, love juice, lower salivation, lube, lubrication, natural, nature's lube, oil of giblets, oil of horn, sexual discharge, sexual secretion, sexual spendings, silky cum, slut butter, twat water, vagina(l) juice, vaginal spendings, vulva sauce, wet, wet deck

Voyeur
gaper, gawker, keek, looker, mixoscopic, peek freak, peeper, peeping tom, peer queer, watch queen, watcher

BIBILOGRAPHY

Aman, Reinhold. *Talking Dirty*. New York: Carrol & Graf Publishers, 1994.

Ayto, John and Simpson, John. *The Oxford Dictionary of Modern Slang*. Oxford: Oxford University Press, 1992.

Baker, Paul. Fantabulosa: *A Dictionary of Polari and Gay Slang*. London: Continuum, 2002.

Butler, Judith. *Gender Trouble: Feminism and the Subversion of Identity*. New York: Routledge, 1990.

Cassell Dictionary of Sex Quotations. London: Cassell, 1993.

Chapman, Robert. *American Slang*. Second Edition. New York: HarperCollins, 1998.

Ellison, M.J. and Fosberry, C.T. *A Queer Companion*. London: Abson Books, 1996.

Ewart, James. *NTC's Dictionary of British Slang and Colloquial Expressions*. Lincolnwood (Chicago), Illinois: NTC/Contemporary Publishing Group, 1997.

Fessler, Jeff and Raunch, Karen. *When Drag is not a Car Race*. New York: Fireside, 1997.

Goldenson, Robert and Anderson, Kenneth. *The Wordsworth Dictionary of Sex*. Ware, Hertfordshire: Wordsworth, 1994.

Green, Jonathon. *The Slang Thesaurus*. London: Penguin Books, 1988.

Green, Jonathon. *Slang Through the Ages*. Illinois: NTC Publishing, 1997.

Guiraud, Pierre. *Dictionnaire. Erotique Editions*. Paris: Payot and Rivages, 1993.

Holder, R.W. Oxford *Dictionary of Euphemisms*. Oxford University Press, 1995.

Johansen, Lenie. *The Penguin Book of Australian Slang*. Victoria: Penguin Books, 1988.

Kipfer, Barbara Ann. *Roget's 21st Century Thesaurus*. New York: Dell Publishing, 1993.

Lewin, Esther and Lewin, Albert E. *The Wordsworth Thesaurus of Slang*. New York: Wordsworth Editions, 1994.

Love, Brenda. *Encyclopedia of Unusual Sex Practices*. Fort Lee: Barricade Books, 1992.

Marcus, Eric. *Making Gay History*. New York: Harper Collins, 2002.

Max, H. *gay(s)language*. Austin: Banned Books, 1988.

Mellie, Roger. *Roger's Profanisaurus*. London: John Brown Publishing, 1988.

The Merriam-Webster Thesaurus. Merriam-Webster Inc. Springfield: Merriam-Webster Inc., 1989.

Nagle, Jill, ed. *Whores and Other Feminists*. New York: Routledge, 1997.

Paterson, R.F. *New Webster's Dictionary and Thesaurus*. Miami: PSI, 1991.

Peterkin, A.D. *The Bald-Headed Hermit and the Artichoke: An Erotic Thesaurus*. Vancouver: Arsenal Pulp Press, 2000.

Richter, Alan. *Sexual Slang*. New York: Harper Perennial, 1993.

Rodgers, Bruce. *Gay Talk: Formerly the Queen's Vernacular*. New York: Paragon Books, 1972.

Scott,Anna and Young, Paul. *Buzzwords LA Freshspeak*. New York: St. Martin's Press, 1997.

Spears, Richard A. *A Dictionary of Slang and Euphemism*. New York: Penguin Books, 1991.

Spignesi, Stephen J. *The Odd Index*. New York: Penguin Books, 1994.

Warner, Michael ed., *Fear of a Queer Planet: Queer Politics and Social Theory*. Minneapolis: Univeristy of Minnesota, 1993.

Williams, Walter L. *The Spirit and the Flesh*. Boston: Beacon Press, 1992.

Websites

Alternate Sources (Trevor Jacques)
Alternate.com/Alternate.html

Barbelith Webzine
www.barbelith.com/

Dictionary of Gay Slang and Historical Terms
www.geocities.com/WestHollywood/Heights/5393/dictionary.html

Dictionary of Gay Terms (Rochester Institute of Technology)
www.rit.edu/~wxygsh/dictionary.html

Flamespeak: The online LGBT dictionary
www.geocities.com/WestHollywood/Cafe/1017/index.html

Gay History and Literature - Essays by Rictor Norton
www.infopt.demon.co.uk/gayhist.htm

In Bed With Fairy Butch
www.planetout.com

Pink Uk's Gay Slang Dictionary
www.pinkuk.com/interests/slang.asp

Queer Slang in the Gay 90s
www.potsdam.edu/clubs/LGBA/pages/other/slang.html

QueerTheory.com
www.queertheory.com

Robin Queen's personal web page
www-personal.umich.edu/~rqueen/PROFESSIONAL/framescv.htm

The Dirty Deed (Charles Panati)
www.bookbuzz.com/panati/dirydeed.htm

The College Slang Page
www.intranet.csupomona.edu/~jasanders/slang

The Gay History of Planet Earth
pages.zoom.co.uk/lgs/gw.html

The London Slang Page
www.geezer.demon.co.uk

National Lesbian & Gay Journalists Association
www.nlgja.org

The Totally Unofficial Rap Dictionary
www.sci.kun.nl/thalia/rapdict

Whoopytestthaupt
http://home.arcor.de/frauenliebe/englwissenlexikon.htm

Wizard's Gay Slang Dictionary
www.hurricane.net/~Wizard/19

GLAD TO BE GAY
WITH BOOKS FROM ARSENAL PULP PRESS

The Bald-Headed Hermit & The Artichoke: An Erotic Thesaurus
A.D. Peterkin
A unique guide to the lingo of sex, by the author of Outbursts and One Thousand Beards.
ISBN 1-55152-063-X; $18.95 Canada/$14.95 US

Brazen Femme: Queering Femininity
Edited by Chloe Brushwood Rose and Anna Camilleri
An anthology of stories, essays, and poems that is a manifesto for the unrepentant lesbian femme. A Lambda Literary Award nominee.
ISBN 1-55152-126-1; $21.95 Canada/$16.95 US

Hot & Bothered 4
Edited by Karen X. Tulchinsky
The latest volume of short short fiction on lesbian desire, in 1,000 words or less. Includes stories by Lesléa Newman, Nisa Donnelly, Shani Mootoo, Tamai Kobayashi, and many more.
ISBN 1-55152-145-8; $19.95 Canada/$15.95 US

One Man's Trash
Ivan E. Coyote
Connected stories about being a dyke in the north; startling in their intimacy, these tales are wry and honest portraits of life, the road, and the spirits within.
ISBN 1-55152-120-2; $16.95 Canada/$13.95 US

One Thousand Beards
Allan Peterkin
The cultural history of facial hair, in all its hirsute guises. Includes style recipes and numerous photographs.
ISBN 1-55152-107-5; $19.95 Canada/$16.95 US

Out/Lines: Underground Gay Graphics from Before Stonewall
Thomas Waugh
A groundbreaking collection of 200 previously unpublished images of gay male sexuality from the queer pre-Stonewall underground. A Lambda Literary Award nominee.
ISBN 1-55152-123-7; $26.95 Canada/$19.95 US

Queer Fear II
Edited by Michael Rowe
A second volume of spine-tingling gay horror fiction, including work by Poppy
Z. Brite, Gemma Files, Nalo Hopkinso, and many more. A Lambda Literary
Award winner.
ISBN 1-55152-122-9; $23.95 Canada/$17.95 US

Quickies 3
Edited by James C. Johnstone
The latest volume of short short fiction on gay male desire, in 1,000 words or
less. Includes stories by Bob Vickery, George K. Ilsley, Daniel Curzon, Michael
V. Smith, and many more.
ISBN 1-55152-144-X; $19.95 Canada/$15.95 US

Quixotic Erotic
Tamai Kobayashi
Step into a world of fantasy and dreams in these beautifully imagined erotic
lesbian tales.
ISBN 1-55152-139-3; $19.95 Canada/$15.95 US

Random Acts of Hatred
George K. Ilsley
In these raw, uncompromising stories, George K. Ilsley explores the thin line
between love and hate, and the outer parameters of desire.
ISBN 1-55152-152-0; $19.95 Canada/$16.95 US

What's Wrong?/What Right?
Edited by Robin Fisher
Two volumes of underground comix (the first explicit, the second general) deal-
ing with the issue of censorship and freedom of speech. Both are fundraisers
for Vancouver's Little Sister's Bookstore.
WW: ISBN 1-55152-136-9; $21.95 Canada/$16.95 US
WR: ISBN 1-55152-137-7; $21.95 Canada/$16.95 US

Books are available at better bookstores, or direct from Arsenal Pulp Press via
our website: *www.arsenalpulp.com*